Charcoal and Cinnamon

Charcoal

Cinnamon

The Politics of Color in Spanish Caribbean Literature

Claudette M. Williams

University Press of Florida

Gainesville · Tallahassee · Tampa · Boca Raton
Pensacola · Orlando · Miami · Jacksonville

05 04 03 02 01 00 6 5 4 3 2 1

Library of Congress Cataloging-in-Publication Data

Williams, Claudette.
Charcoal and cinnamon: the politics of color in Spanish Caribbean
literature / Claudette M. Williams.
p. cm.
Includes bibliographical references (p.   -   ) and index.
ISBN 0-8130-1736-X (cloth: alk. paper)
1. Caribbean literature (Spanish)—History and criticism. 2. Women,
black, in literature. 3. Race relations in literature. I. Title.
PQ7361.W48 1999
860.9'9287'089960729—dc21 99-43663

The University Press of Florida is the scholarly publishing agency
for the State University System of Florida, comprising Florida
A & M University, Florida Atlantic University, Florida International
University, Florida State University, University of Central Florida,
University of Florida, University of North Florida, University of
South Florida, and University of West Florida.

University Press of Florida
15 Northwest 15th Street
Gainesville, FL 32611-2079
http://www.upf.com

To the memory of my mother, who gave me her eyes to see

For my daughters, Kamilah and Shari

For Coreen, my generous and ever-understanding sister

CONTENTS

PREFACE

This book explores changing ideas about what it means to be black or mulatto and female in the Caribbean. It brings together the work of Caribbean writers, both male and female, and looks at the ways in which they have used language to represent and to distinguish women of African ethnic origin. Various studies have been written on this subject, but in much of the existing research, there is a blindness to the literature of the non-English-speaking territories. This tendency stands out in the recent work on Caribbean women writers, in which contributions from the French and Spanish islands either are missing or occupy a marginal place. This is partly the result of a lack of agreement about the geographical constitution of the region. Many studies imply a view of the Caribbean as restricted to the numerically dominant Anglophone territories. Some researchers have further encouraged the exclusion of the Spanish-speaking islands by using language and political history as the criteria for treating Hispanic Caribbean literatures as part of a Latin or Spanish American corpus.

There is, however, sufficient justification for seeing these islands, despite their peculiarities, as belonging to the broader Caribbean cultural matrix. Indeed some studies have reached across the linguistic divide to develop the appropriate historical, cultural, and ideological linkages between these three Caribbean language areas. Notable among them are G. R. Coulthard's *Race and Colour in Caribbean Literature* (1962); Selwyn Cudjoe's *Resistance and Caribbean Literature* (1980) and his edition of critical essays, *Caribbean Women Writers* (1990); Gordon K. Lewis's *Main Currents in Caribbean Thought* (1983); and *Caribbean Currents: Caribbean Music from Rumba to Reggae* (1995), by Peter Manuel in collaboration with Kenneth Bilby and Michael Largey. Carole Boyce Davies and Elaine Savory Fido in *Out of the Kumbla: Caribbean Women and Litera-*

ture (1990) and more recently Silvio Torres-Saillant in *Caribbean Poetics: Toward an Aesthetic of West Indian Literature* (1997) have also promoted this vision of the unity of Caribbean literature.

Some anthologies invite such a unitary view of the Caribbean literary domain. These include Pamela María Smorkaloff's *If I Could Write This in Fire: An Anthology of Literature from the Caribbean* (1994) and *Her True-True Name: An Anthology of Women's Writing from the Caribbean*, a 1989 anthology of short fiction, in which Pamela Mordecai and Elizabeth Wilson have brought together works written originally in English and English translations of French and Spanish authors. Current movements toward economic collaboration among Haiti, Cuba, the Dominican Republic, and the community of English-speaking Caribbean nations also signal the potential for the strengthening of union in the cultural sphere.

The shared experience of colonialism and the subsequent crusade for decolonization, which mark the history of all Caribbean societies, are the factors that, to a large extent, have shaped literary responses in the region. Not surprisingly, the work of writers from the different geographical locations exhibits a fundamental unity of sentiment and vision, and certain motifs recur in their depictions of women of African descent. But the distinct nuances in the representational practices of these writers also reflect the variations in the history and experience of the people of the different Caribbean regions.

With this book my purpose is to broaden the existing body of gender-centered Caribbean studies by inserting the literature of the hitherto marginalized Spanish-speaking islands, noting its intersection with the literatures of the Anglophone and Francophone territories. The scope of the study extends from the beginnings of a distinguishable Caribbean literary tradition in the nineteenth century to the 1970s. I have singled out the major representational trends as well as unique creations. The critical focus centers not only on the images as they appear in finished form, but equally on their historical contexts, the ideas and values that have shaped them, the processes by which they have been constructed, and the political functions they have served. My aim, ultimately, is to explore the complex and dynamic interaction between ideological contexts, on the one hand, and cultural projects, on the other. I will not pretend to be engaging in an ideologically neutral reading of this literature, nor are my interpretations formulated in an authoritarian mode. What this book offers the reader is one insider's response to the intricacies of racial and gender politics as they are played out in the literary domain.

Charcoal and cinnamon are two of the racial metaphors used to refer to black and mulatto women in Cuba's classic nineteenth-century novel *Cecilia Valdés,* by Cirilo Villaverde. In acknowledging white men's favoring of the *mulata* over the black woman, Leonardo, the principal white male character, informs his friend: "If that is your way of saying you do not like cinnamon, then too bad for you Pancho, for it means that you prefer charcoal, a type that is inferior by far" (I:192–93). At stake in this oblique reference is the white ruling-class concern with racial hierarchy in Cuban slave society. The absolute supremacy of whiteness and the inferiority of nonwhiteness were assumed to be unquestionable. But in social life people of mixed African ancestry and those of full African origin were not collapsed into a single racial group.

As hinted at by Villaverde's metaphors, the *mulata*'s supposed racial advantage was used to elevate her above the black woman. As cinnamon is more appealing than charcoal, so too was the mulatto woman's perceived aesthetic and sensual attraction more esteemed than the mere utility value imputed to the black woman. Writers in nineteenth-century Cuba accorded some literary status to the *mulata* (even while they preserved the society's white supremacist values); in the same period the black woman was, at best, not representable and, at worst, anathema. This colonial discrimination has appeared under different guises and in varying degrees at subsequent stages of the Caribbean region's literary history.

In exploring these representations I have made primary selections from published works from Cuba, Puerto Rico, and the Dominican Republic. Unless otherwise indicated, translations of the Spanish texts are my own. My selections include examples that form part of mainstream literary conventions and also those that are eccentric, from both canonized and less well known authors. I have opted for depth of analysis of certain works while referring in less detail to others belonging to the same context. This choice is dictated to some extent by historical circumstance. In these Spanish territories fewer women write and publish than men, and the preferred modes for writers of both sexes are poetry and the short story. Literary interest in people of African ancestry was far greater in Cuba than in Puerto Rico and the Dominican Republic during the nineteenth century. Although various affinities of language, culture, and history link these three territories, the peculiarities of each limit the extent of the generalizations to be made about them.

The book had its genesis in work that I undertook as a graduate student at Stanford University. I soon came to realize that the subject held more than mere academic interest for me; it spoke to my own lived experience as an Afro-Caribbean woman. In the intervening years since the beginning of this project, I have been able to explore the literature of the other language areas of the region. This opportunity has afforded me a more globally Caribbean perspective, the broader context necessary for expanding that original research into this book. This study owes much to the critical work already carried out by many scholars in Caribbean studies and is intended for readers with an interest in the sociology of the arts and for others with a special interest in comparative Caribbean literary studies.

I acknowledge a large debt of gratitude to the supervisors of my original research: Professor Mary Louise Pratt, who showed great rigor in her critical comments and equal generosity in her encouragement; Professor Sylvia Wynter, who helped me to maintain a firm Caribbean focus, and from whose vast knowledge of, and enthusiastic interest in, the field I benefited greatly; and Professor Tomás Ybarra Frausto, who offered very useful advice, especially regarding other contexts to which my study is related. I am also grateful to my colleagues at the Mona campus of the University of the West Indies, who have been vigilant in following the book's progress and urging its completion. I must also thank the University Press of Florida team of Susan Fernandez and Gillian Hillis for the efficiency and gentleness with which they have guided me through the publication process. A final word of thanks is due to the LASPAU organization, through whose agency and funding I was able to carry out a large part of the initial research.

Introduction

The identity of Caribbean people of African descent, defined originally by those to whom they were subordinated, has been constantly redefined with the changing modes of coexistence in Caribbean society since slavery. This process is clearly inscribed in the portrayal of black and mulatto women in the literature of the region. A seminal part of any discussion of these representations is an understanding of the Western artistic tradition that institutionalized specific ways of viewing and representing people of African extraction. Of equal importance to the image-making process are the nature of the historical encounter of Africa and Europe in the Caribbean, the social relations that have resulted from this experience, and the impact of various political movements and changes in the social order.

Popular perception of the status, role, and destiny of three of the racial categories of women in the ex-colonies of Latin America and the Caribbean is condensed in the well-known saying "the white woman for marriage, the mulatto woman for a good time, and the black woman for work." This paradigm echoes the distinction between white "ladies," brown "favourites," and black "wenches" noted by Barbara Bush (1981) in her study of British Caribbean slave society. The color-class hierarchy reflected in these classifications has persisted, with some modification, in the present. More specifically, the two models confirm that race and sexuality have been widely accepted as prime contexts for the representation of these women. They also indicate that race determines both the general sexualization of dark-skinned women and the differentiated sexualization of black and mulatto women.

The white woman, descendant of the European colonizer, is idolized and prized as the sexless model of purity and beauty. The light-skinned mulatto or brown woman, hybrid product of the sexual liaisons between European men and African women, represents the Creole middle group, but is tainted racially, and, by extension, morally. Therefore she can only be the provider of those taboo sexual pleasures that would tarnish the "fair lady." The black-skinned woman, clearest descendant of the African slave, occupies the lowest end of the social scale. In the Spanish saying she retains the labor value of her slave past, but like her white counterpart, she is divested of her sexuality, though for different social reasons. Both the denial of her sexuality in the first saying and the ascription to her of the role of wench or prostitute in the second bespeak the stigma that has been attached to the black woman's race.

Yet even these classifications do not tell the full story of the many nuances in the racial and gender politics of the Caribbean. Despite her higher standing in the socio-racial order, the white woman has been an infrequent source of inspiration for the majority of Caribbean writers. Black and mulatto women, on the other hand, have commanded the interest of a remarkable number of writers of different racial backgrounds.

Spanish Caribbean literature is indissociably linked to the major moments in Caribbean history: slavery and colonialism, nationalist movements, the ideological culture of the post–World War II era, and the 1959 Cuban Revolution and the cultural politics that it engendered. I have placed the representations into four main (and sometimes overlapping) categories within this historical framework. In the first group are those depictions in which the focus is on physical and racial characteristics. My interpretation of the aesthetic value judgments inherent in these portrayals takes as its starting point the historical attitudes to race and color that have informed the perceptions of nonwhite women. Writers exhibit varying, and often contradictory, responses to the women's race and color, ranging from obsession with those features that distinguish them physically, to ethnocentric perceptions of them as aesthetically inferior by white standards; from aesthetic vindication to portrayals in which their racial properties are seen as incidental; from Romantic idealization to feelings of contempt.

Constituting the second group are those representations in which the emphasis is on sexuality and which can be traced back to the literature of the nineteenth century. This image gained its widest currency in the 1920s and 1930s, when it was inflated and disseminated extensively by the creators of *negrista* verse. Also located in this context is the third category of images proceeding from the search for national identity and cultural uniqueness, which some writers expressed by appropriating the mulatto woman as the supreme icon of the Caribbean. This development occurred within the broader framework of discussions about miscegenation and creolization—two prominent subjects in Caribbean discourse in the nineteenth and early twentieth centuries.

Depictions of the woman of African descent as a historical subject and as a human individual comprise the fourth representational mode. Though frequently separated in time and distinguished by the authors' choice of expressive method, the representations that fall into this class are united by their explicit location of the Afro-Caribbean woman in her historical context. Whether the technique used is documentary or dramatic, whether the author foregrounds objective social situation or subjective inner world, this perspective, often the province of female authors, offers a more profound insight into her lived experience.

Sociocultural and racial considerations are related parts of the framework for analyzing Caribbean literature and the writers' relation to their subject matter. Often the author, the written text, and the reader share a common social space in the dominant culture, while the reality of the socially marginalized people they write about falls outside this sphere. The dynamics of this relationship of distance is a notable determinant in the process of literary production. On the other hand, the author's race, which is one variable governing perception and ideological orientation, needs to be approached with some caution. The reason for this is that, although racial divisions characterize Caribbean societies, racial ideologies, like race itself, do not confine themselves within neatly defined boundaries. Cultural conditioning is often as crucial a factor as race.

Another reflection of the complexity of the race issue in the literature is the paradoxical expression of antiblack prejudice by blacks and mulattoes, who have absorbed the white supremacist ideology. I have also avoided the assumption that those representations that arise out of the racial experience of Afro-Caribbean authors have automatic validity, or that depictions by authors without a claim to African ancestry are of necessity inauthentic. My focus, therefore, is less on the race of the writer and more on his or her attitude to race, on the race consciousness that controls the literary voice where this seems relevant. Such an acknowledgment does not constitute, however, the denial of a possible correlation between a given author's racial identity, on the one hand, and his or her literary practice and ideology, on the other. Notable differences separate the vision of Cuban poet Nicolás Guillén, who is mulatto, from that of Puerto Rico's Luis Palés Matos, who is white.

Another practice that I have sought to avoid is the privileging of "good" literature over "bad" literature. My main purpose is to dismantle the diverse images and stereotypes of women of African descent generated by the literary tradition of the Hispanic Caribbean. An exploration of how the images are constructed will also disclose their assumptions, contradictions, and hidden meanings. This methodology does not demand the establishment of a hierarchy of aesthetic value. Whether a work's ideological dimension is dominant or seems subordinated to aesthetic imperatives, ideological criticism has relevance for the reading of all literary works. All writers, to some degree, are concerned with positive self-presentation, adequate self-expression, and effective persuasion. My concern is with the strategies they use for these ends.

The meanings of literary texts do not remain eternally fixed in the historical moment in which they appear. Each subsequent reader or reading will also generate new meanings. This study has been a voyage of self-exploration. My own experience and position as an Afro-Caribbean woman have influenced my critical perceptions in no small measure. In many instances, my separation from the writers' ideology facilitates an essentially skeptical approach to the interpretation of the texts.

Literary Discourse and Ideology

Literary studies in recent times have moved away from the view of literary works as finished products to contemplate what is involved in the process of their production and the process of their reception and interpretation. Literary language has come to be regarded as discourse. Discourse is language seen from the perspective of its use, produced by a speaker or writer, and addressed, albeit implicitly, to a reader or listener. The literary text may seem to be a one-way mode of communication, but the very act of reading makes of the reader a silent, though not necessarily passive, participant in the communication process. An active relationship exists between writers and their communities; the text is a vehicle of communication between the writer and an implicit interlocutor as well as a larger community of readers.

Literary discourse, like all human actions, is a product, determined by both individual and social factors that may complement or conflict with each other. Literary creation is also a practice—that is, it is a response to, an interpretation or transposition of, real situations. As such, it plays a mediating role, serving to illuminate or obscure reality and to legitimize or subvert existing social structures. While this perspective of literature as discourse gives primacy to the author as producer, it does not rest solely on authorial intention. Intention is an important consideration, but achievement does not conform inevitably to objective.

This study applies the theory of art as social and ideological activity to the analysis of literary practice. In the ensuing discussions I refer sometimes to the specific definition of *ideology* as an explicit and codified set of ideas informing some social, economic, or political theory (as in feminist or Marxist ideology). This constitutes what may be referred to as "conscious" ideology. In the second and more general sense, the term refers to the manner of thinking characteristic of a class or individual. Marxist literary critic Terry Eagleton has expanded on this second meaning and defined *ideology* in broad terms as "the largely *concealed* structure of values which informs and underlies our factual statements," and as "the ways in which what we say and believe connects with the power-structure and power-relations of the society we live in" (14; my emphasis). Such beliefs, though deeply entrenched, often function in unconscious ways. It is this notion of hidden or unconscious ideology that I will engage in much of my interpretation.

Marxist theory has given a distinctive stamp to the notion of ideology. Attitudes and values, according to this theory, are not idiosyncratic, but relate to, and are expressive of, economic structure, class interests, and conflicts. Thus conceived, ideology is the medium through which the individual is made to relate to particular social power systems. In classical Marxist theory the dominant ideology functions mainly as a means of presenting as natural that which is, in effect, socially constructed. It ensures the survival of existing social structures. Nevertheless, one must also take into account the possible coexistence of alternative, conflicting, and even subversive ideologies within a given social order. Literary discourses, like the social formations out of which they arise, are not inevitably homogeneous.

Specific discourses exist and can be expressed because they derive from prior belief systems or ideologies, so that ideology is always embedded in and, in fact, determines discourse. The task of identifying connections between the literary text and social and ideological structures poses a hazard, since to some extent it is a practice based on intuition. Although it will be possible to show, in many instances, the connection between the values expressed in a representation and certain social ideologies, it cannot be assumed that all values may be thus categorized. Cultural practices and social ideologies or political projects relate to each other not monolithically but in a multifaceted and symbiotic manner; they intersect in different ways. Cultural practices may be conceived of as simply the products and the reflectors of social values. However, they often actively constitute, endorse, or, more subversively, overturn these values. It is also necessary to go beyond the classical Marxist emphasis on class divisions and class conflict as the chief determinants of ideology to consider other social causes. With specific reference to Caribbean societies, any mechanistic application of this theory would be reductive, since these societies are characteristically stratified along racial as well as class lines.

In the Caribbean, race is primarily a matter of skin color with other associated physical features (e.g., the texture of the hair, the shape of the nose, and the size of lips). Good looks, as popularly defined, correlate with the proximity of the individual's racial features to the Caucasian phenotype. Hence mulattoes rank above blacks in the aesthetic hierarchy. Color mediates social relations and arrangements and is inextricably bound up with understandings of personal identity. In *Crick Crack, Monkey* Trinidadian novelist Merle Hodge exposes the intractable discrimination practiced within the Afro-Caribbean community, where light-skinned women are favored over black women. This novel provides insight into the ways in which the obsession with skin shade distinctions vitiates family relationships: "In particular, Auntie Beatrice seemed to blame Jessica on Uncle Norman. '. . . it's not any fault of mine that you are dark; you just have to take one look at me and you will see that! What you don't have in looks you have to make up for otherwise!'" (82–83). Aunt Beatrice constructs Jessica's blackness as a reproach; it represents an absence for which Jessica can only compensate by other means.

The tenacity of the colonial heritage is apparent in a class structure in which light or white skin color generally accompanies upper-class standing as much as darkness does lower-class status. However, the link between ethnic identity and class membership is not a monolithic one. Race is not exclusively a chromatic category. Culture is another factor that often mediates race relations, but even cultural unity does not erase racial discrimination. Race is understandably therefore a major constituent of Caribbean discourse. Literary texts articulate race and color issues sometimes at the level of explicit theme and more often implicitly in the subtext of other discourses.

Yet another of the recognized inadequacies of orthodox Marxism as an explanatory theory is its ignoring of inequitable gender divisions and women's oppression as elementary features of most societies. The very subject of this study requires that we consider the ideological construction of gender and, more precisely, the depictions of women that masculinist ideology has normalized. Spanish Caribbean writers, for example, have shown a characteristic interest in black female sexuality while they de-emphasize the sexual dimension in their portrayals of black men. Besides, much of the field of Caribbean literary production has been controlled historically by male writers. With the recent increase in the number of visible female writers and the insights offered by the various currents of feminist thought, it is possible to undertake more gender-conscious readings of this literature.

It is necessary, nonetheless, to question the appropriateness of totalizing feminist theories for contexts such as the Caribbean. Most Caribbean feminists would feel discomfort with the tendency of some Eurocentered feminists to ignore or de-emphasize race in their gender analyses. What is needed, therefore, is not an approach that entails either wholesale adoption or dogmatic rejection of the dominant versions of feminism (i.e., its Anglo-American and European forms), but a disposition to consider the implications of these theories for the Caribbean experience and to modify them, where necessary, to suit the local reality.

Racial divisions complicate gender divisions in Caribbean societies. Nonwhiteness is not conceived of as an undifferentiated racial category. Homogenizing labels such as "women of color" or "women of African descent" are used infrequently in everyday discourse. Women who are perceived to be of full or predominantly African ancestry are commonly referred to as "black" (negra), while "mulatto" or "brown" are terms applied to those who are perceived to be of an African and European mixture. The common roots of these women are generally of less consequence than the distinctions that are normally used to separate them. What mediates the discourse on their sexuality, for example, is the perception of the color difference between black and brown Afro-Caribbean women. I have therefore based my analysis of the various representations on the understanding that the social divisions arise out of the interaction of at least three variables: race, gender, and class. Within this intricate web it is the insidious presence of race and color that gives a distinctive stamp to Caribbean discourse.

Deconstruction is now established as one of the most fruitful ways of reading literary works. Underlying this critical method is the premise that the literary text is an ideological construct and can therefore be *de-*

constructed. Deconstructive analysis seeks to illuminate the multiple meanings of a literary text and the internal contradictions that frequently underlie its surface coherence. Catherine Belsey's explanation of the nature and function of a dominant ideology highlights this fundamental premise of deconstructive critical practice: "Ideology obscures the real conditions of existence by presenting partial truths. It is a set of omissions, gaps rather than lies, smoothing over contradictions, appearing to provide answers to questions which in reality it evades, and masquerading as coherence in the interests of the social relations generated by and necessary to the reproduction of the existing mode of production" (57). Armed with this premise, the reader can unmask the ideology of the text, and by probing its subtextual layers, release unintended meanings, silences, and ambiguities. The reader can discover the means by which the text constructs its reality and the writer's use of specific strategies to conceal as much as to reveal attitudes and values. One must frequently examine the assumptions and implications of both the omissions and the emphases of a particular representation to arrive at an adequate understanding of its significance. For example, portrayals of the Afro-Caribbean woman as inferior may bespeak an obviously racist stance. But even ostensibly favorable representations may contain residual prejudices.

It is more useful to view many of the postures the writers assume as influenced by existing social values rather than as idiosyncratic. The images they create are rarely of intrinsic value; they are frequently pressed into some ideological service. This has not always been a spontaneous development, for at different times Caribbean governments have deliberately fostered the use of culture to promote political causes. But, the obviously politicized images apart, some seemingly apolitical (or nonpolitical) representations of women of African descent imply political motives and complicity with particular ideologies. Changes in the perception of people of African descent are often responses to changes in the social and ideological domains. Spanish Caribbean literature has been deeply implicated in this process. In depicting the Afro-Caribbean woman, writers are responding to a social context.

The deconstructive approach also recognizes the fact that the act of reading is not ideology free. Like the author, the reader assumes a specific position in relation to the text, its ideology, and the reality it creates. In the act of reading, the reader *produces* the work's meanings. The participation of the reader adds a dialogic dimension to the literary process; meaning in a text derives from the dialogue between the author's voice and the reader's consciousness. Both the production and the interpretation of literary texts are ideologically determined. The deconstructive critic's effort to denaturalize a work's ideology will be facilitated by a distancing of the critic from that ideology. Such an acknowledgment of the subjective nature of the act of reading precludes the imposition of determinate meanings on the text. My aim, therefore, is not to dictate definitive meanings but to suggest some of the more compelling ways of interpreting the purposes and effects of these literary representations.

In his discussion of the discourse of power, Roger Fowler asserts that "[language] is an instrument for consolidating and manipulating concepts and relationships in the area of power and control (as well as other areas of social and ideological structure). . . . The use of language continuously constitutes the statuses and roles upon which people base their claim to exercise power, and the statuses and roles which seem to require subservience. Language is a reality-creating social practice" ("Power," 61–62). This formulation may be readily applied, in many instances, to the image-making process of which the Afro-Caribbean woman is subject, and especially to the many stereotypes of this figure that recur in the literature being studied.

The relationship between stereotypes and reality is a complex one. It is important to note, in the first place, that stereotypes frequently have some basis, albeit remote, in sociological fact. But the evolution of a stereotype usually involves exaggerating observed traits and extending impressions about individuals to the whole class to which those individuals belong. Direct contact or personal experience rarely informs the stereotypes held by most people. They more often acquire these indirectly through informal social discourse. Not only are stereotypes pervasive, but they also prove resistant to change. In the face of evidence that "disproves" the stereotype, the holder will tend to regard the case as an exception. Thus formed and fixed, stereotypes inevitably influence reality.

Stereotypes of people of African extraction have evolved out of a specific system of power relations in which dominant white groups have constituted them as inferior, and thereby sought to give legitimacy to the notion of white racial superiority. The inferiority complex long experienced by blacks is explainable in these terms. Stereotypes encourage particular types of social action and interaction. This function can be seen in the same light as the view expressed by Marxist ideologue Louis Althusser. He theorizes that in class society the reproduction of labor power requires "a reproduction of submission to the ruling ideology for the workers and a reproduction of the ability to manipulate the ruling ideology correctly for the agents of exploitation and repression, so that they, too, will provide for the domination of the ruling class 'in words'" (127–28).

Assimilation of stereotypical images of themselves has served to entrap blacks in their inferior status. Erna Brodber advances this view in her documentation of some stereotypes of the Caribbean woman. She believes that these can "affect her role performance, adaptive strategies and her status" (2). In *Black Skin, White Masks,* Martinican theorist Frantz Fanon also explains the mulatto woman's psychic alienation as a consequence of her internalization of antiblack prejudice and of her desire to be white. Not only do stereotypes play a mediating role in social interaction, but they often displace and substitute for reality. Even if they do not invent stereotypes, formal discourse genres, such as literature, often incorporate and so institutionalize them. Caribbean writers' greater proximity to their subjects accounts for some of the differences between their depictions of blacks and those of other writers. But this has not been sufficient to eliminate the tendency among the former to reproduce or create stereotypes of the woman of African descent.

Discussion of the literary representations of the Afro-Caribbean woman needs to take into account the writer's relation to the historical moment and to the artistic tradition in which he or she works. Another important consideration is the extent to which the writer's perceptions are shaped by the ideology of the dominant culture, or by alternative ideologies. Colonialism had naturalized a view of the world that ensured the integration of the woman of African descent into the society at subordinate levels. In the hegemonic discourse of Western literature, she had appeared as an inferior subject. Caribbean writers have created images of her that either confirm or contest this hegemonic discourse. A study of the discursive strategies associated with these images requires a consideration of the historical and ideological contexts in which they have been constructed.

The Literary-Ideological Map

Some amount of unevenness marks the evolution of the literature of the different Caribbean territories. This has resulted from the variations in the colonial systems organized by the different European powers and from the differences in political status and in the pace of political development, particularly the achievement of independence. Nevertheless, there is considerable similarity in the pattern of development and in the themes of the literatures of the Spanish, French, and English Caribbean. In the eighteenth century the tendency among these writers (generally white Creoles) was to avert their gaze from local reality and from the Negro, in particular. During the nineteenth century a number of these writers began to focus on their local situation, but viewed it through foreign lenses. Submission to the European literary tradition is the characteristic feature of creative Caribbean writing during slavery and the colonial period.

The process of Caribbeanization of literary culture has been a gradual one and is intimately bound up with the growth of national consciousness. In Haiti, for example, where the slave-led revolt resulted in the gaining of early independence in 1804, the will to incorporate local subjects and to validate local culture can be discerned in some nineteenth-century writings. A sense of national awareness is also evident in Spanish Caribbean literature by the second half of the nineteenth century, especially in Cuba and, to a lesser extent, in Puerto Rico. In the English-speaking countries, the majority of which gained political independence after 1960, this development was more tardy, beginning to appear clearly only in the first half of the twentieth century. This explains why, for example, nineteenth-century Haitian literature depicts the woman of African descent more frequently than the literature of the Anglophone Caribbean of the same period. In all cases, however, the development of national awareness has expressed itself through the will of the producers of literary culture to release the Caribbean mind from the tyranny of inherited European modes of perception and representation. This common objective has generated a diverse range of literary modalities for the representation of the Afro-Caribbean woman.

Black and mulatto women make their first appearance as important figures in the nineteenth-century Cuban novels of slavery. Some of these feature prominent black or mulatto female protagonists from whom the novels take their titles (*Petrona y Rosalía* [1838], *Cecilia Valdés* [1839, 1882]), and even in those whose slave protagonists are male, black and mulatto women have significant roles (*Francisco* [1839], *El negro Francisco* [1873]). The novelists' main concern was less the slaves themselves and more the evils of slavery, and they aimed their works at reform rather than abolition of the system. Yet they reveal, incidentally, a great deal about the way nineteenth-century society perceived nonwhites, and they created a pattern for the representation of these women that became a blueprint for many subsequent writers.

After about the middle of the nineteenth century, Cuban poets also began to fashion an image of the *mulata,* initially with very vague contours and shaped in the then-dominant Romantic mold. Gradually, some writers of the period began to discern the locally distinctive characteristics of her identity and to add native elements to the inherited discourse. This was one of the early signs of a process of cultural differentiation that heralded the making of a nationalist tradition. Many divergences are apparent between the nineteenth-century treatment of Afro-Caribbean women and that of literary works of the post-1920 period. But it is also important to recognize that the images of black and mulatto women disseminated at the beginning of the twentieth century had their antecedents in the earlier period.

Afro-Caribbean people became increasingly involved in the struggle for independence and eventually for the end of their bondage in the nineteenth century. As they assumed new political roles and, in many instances, forced social transformation, so they came to be viewed differently. National consciousness, which had started to emerge in the nineteenth century, gained vigor in the first decades of the twentieth century. One of the most important tasks that postcolonial writers have set themselves is to relieve the Afro-Caribbean woman of the historical stigma attached to her blackness. They attempted this at first through timid statements affirming her difference from her white European counterpart. Later writers have made bolder and more confident assertions of her intrinsic racial and aesthetic validity.

Increasingly after the 1920s, writers of the region began to incorporate Afro-Caribbean themes into their work and to formulate theories of cultural identity. In the Spanish Caribbean this process brought blacks and mulattoes into the center of a literary movement. *Negrismo* has been one of the most significant literary expressions of cultural nationalism in the literature of the Spanish Caribbean. It has produced a large body of poems portraying Afro-Caribbean people in their sociocultural milieu. Among these, the Afro-Caribbean woman, black or mulatto, is a remarkable figure. The movement found its most vigorous expression in Cuba and Puerto Rico. It was less vibrant in the Dominican Republic, where the relatively marginal interest in the African heritage has traditionally been a function of that country's wish to project a white identity.

Negrismo has been associated with the Negrophilism that was born out of the antirationalist ethos of post–World War Europe and that manifested itself in the cult of the primitive and the exaltation of the life of the senses.

But while this international vogue might have impelled the local movement, it seems that political developments in the region also made their ideological impact on literary production. *Negrismo* emerged out of a heightened awareness in the 1920s that the African element is part of what gives Caribbean life its distinctive character. Besides, it expressed the desire to differentiate the new national self from the former colonizer and became, after the 1898 Spanish American war, the locally grown response to the threat of American imperialism.

Initially *negrista* poetry was hailed for capturing and thereby validating the Afro-Caribbean cultural ethos, and for being more sincere and authentic than its European counterpart. But the movement did not entail unequivocal improvement in the literary representation of the Negro. In fact, it may even be true to say that it helped to consolidate old negative stereotypes and introduce new and equally undesirable ones. *Negrista* representations of the Afro-Caribbean experience frequently betrayed prejudiced attitudes in the writers, and, especially in the early phase, poets like Luis Palés Matos, Ramón Guirao, José Tallet, Emilio Ballagas, and Manuel del Cabral merely perpetuated the myth of the Negro as an exotic, instinct-driven, and nonintellectual being. It is in this climate that Spanish Caribbean poets cultivated the image of the black woman as a sensationally sexual creature, an image that lost its potency but survived the decline of the movement after the 1930s.

Miscegenation and creolization have been abiding concerns of Caribbean writers and intellectuals in their attempts to define national identity. Nineteenth-century literary discourse betrays the society's deep disquiet with the racially hybrid mulatto group, which it perceived as a threat to white supremacy. Representations of the *mulata* in this context imply ideological resistance to racial mixing. In the Spanish territories the explicit promotion of a national identity based on racial and cultural unity is a phenomenon of the early twentieth century. But this version of nationalist discourse avoids both African and European atavism. Writers choose instead to constitute national identity in terms of transculturation—that is, as an interactive process in which the original foreign participants (Africa and Europe) have produced an indigenous hybrid race and culture. Even the affirmation of the African heritage by a writer such as the Afro-Cuban Nicolás Guillén does not preclude this ideology of racial integration. Writers from the English-speaking territories have also articulated this discourse of racial and cultural synthesis, especially after the mid-twentieth century.

Spanish Caribbean poetry has distinguished itself by appropriating the figure of the *mulata* as the symbol of national identity and racial integration. Yet some of this poetry reflects the fact that although *mulatez* is invoked in the literary definitions of national character, and despite official claims of racial tolerance or neutrality, racist ideology is perpetuated in subtle ways. In the 1920s, nationalist zeal and the desire for unity often obscured or distorted national reality. In general, nationalist fervor created a climate more conducive to rhetorical forms and symbolism than to confrontation of social reality.

Its advocacy of *mulatez* as the national ideal is a fundamental point of ideological divergence between *negrismo* and *négritude*, its equivalent in Francophone Caribbean literature. *Négritude* writers rejected the European heritage, vindicated black cultural values, and favored black cultural autonomy. Martinican poet Aimé Césaire, for example, was as antimulatto as he was antiwhite, because of his perception of the common bourgeois character of both racial groups. In the Spanish-speaking Caribbean, however, *negrista* writers have reproduced, for the most part, an official ideology defining national identity in terms of an African-European synthesis. One may understand this promotion of a hybrid Caribbean identity as born of a political desire to foster national harmony. But like the earlier antislavery novels, when viewed in a more suspicious light, this project, in its preoccupation with the national profile, betrays lack of concern for the real-life condition of blacks and mulattoes.

As a consequence of the ideological developments arising out of the Second World War, Caribbean literature assumed an increasingly social orientation. By this time the Afro-Caribbean woman had been firmly established as a literary icon. But even before this time, some writers, usually of African descent, had begun to reject the dominant stereotypes and to present a more profound and complex view of her reality. They chose to foreground, with critical intent, the human and social dimensions of the Afro-Caribbean woman's experience.

In the specific case of Cuba, the socialist ideology of the 1959 Revolution engendered new discourses for the definition of the Afro-Caribbean woman. In the literature produced in the early postrevolution era, the ideological imperative assumes dominance. Both those writers who support and those who oppose the Castro regime reflect this tendency. Among writers who support the revolution the dominant class perspective of Marxist theory has displaced the ethno-racial emphasis of cultural nationalism. This is borne out in Nicolás Guillén's postrevolution view of *negrismo*. He associates antiblack racism with Cuba's presocialist past: "before the Revolution, *Négritude* or *Negrismo* could be explained as . . . a manifestation of the class struggle. But when a revolution eliminates that struggle and gives power to the working class without regard to skin color, that notion of superiority or racial differentiation disappears" (Morejón, *Recopilación de textos* 44–45). But even in the guarded tone of Guillén's comment one discerns idealism rather than assertion of fact. His claim has been strongly challenged inside and outside Cuba by those who have disclosed the insidious presence of racism in that socialist state. (See, for example, Clytus, *Black Man in Red Cuba*, and Moore, "Cuba: The Untold Story" and "Congo or Carabalí? Race Relations in Socialist Cuba.") Aline Helg's recent study on the Afro-Cuban political struggle has properly contextualized the myth of Cuba as a raceless and classless society. It perpetuates, in her view, the ideology that has been used effectively since the late nineteenth century to preempt Afro-Cuban dissent.

The strengthening of the feminist movement since the 1970s has placed gender on the Caribbean cultural and political agenda. It has resulted in increased attention to the work of women writers and to the expression of gender issues through the various media. In this regard, Spanish Caribbean women writers, though forming a minority, have been the leaders of a transgressive enterprise that has altered the boundaries of the region's literary tradition. They have promoted images that serve to challenge, displace, or offer alternatives to the entrenched representations.

1

"The nice one . . . and the other one"
The Discourse of Race and Color

Writing in 1962, G. R. Coulthard made the following claim about the representation of black and mulatto women in Caribbean literature: "if one looks into the literature of those Caribbean countries where a more or less great percentage of the population is coloured, it becomes abundantly clear that not only is the coloured woman, black or mulatto, presented in a favourable aesthetic light, but the subject of her beauty is so frequent as to be a commonplace throughout the literature of the whole area" (*Race,* 87). While this statement may be valid for the specific texts that Coulthard chose as illustrations, it is also a potentially misleading generalization, one that glosses over the many subtle variations and ambiguities in these representations.

This chapter takes its title from Beatriz's description of her sisters in Trinidadian novelist Merle Hodge's *Crick Crack, Monkey:* "Oh the nice one is Carol, the fairskin' one; and the other one is Jessica" (80). This description captures more accurately than Coulthard's statement the skin shade discrimination that is the essence of the racial dynamic of Caribbean societies. A deeply entrenched antiblack racism, such as Hodge's fictional character expresses, was one of the insidious ideological consequences of Caribbean slavery. Slavery, of course, was not a uniquely European creation. What was distinctive about its transatlantic form was that the Negro's supposed racial inferiority was used as its defense. Caribbean slave society was organized on the dual basis of a master/slave and a white/black polarity.

The origins of the race-color question can be traced back to the first contact of European travelers with Africans. Europeans defined Africans in terms of their color difference, and made the black "Other" into the negative antithesis of a notionally ideal white "Self." Differences of degree and expression aside, racial prejudice against blacks and a sense of their own racial superiority had infected all the European colonizing powers. Terry Eagleton notes that a characteristic of ideology is the practice of seeing things in binary opposition (113). Slavery's racist ideology is a classic example of this theory. It set rigid boundaries between whiteness and its alleged opposite, blackness, and deemed the black slaves inferior to their white masters in culture and intelligence, in physical appearance and skin color. Whiteness was accepted as the ideal, the reference point for the aesthetic disparagement of blacks. With the emergence of the mulatto class, slave society created a color spectrum as the basis for the assigning of positions in the Caribbean's racial hierarchy. In the pigmentocracy, brown-skinned mulattoes (a closer approximation of the unchallenged white aesthetic ideal) occupied a position above black-skinned Negroes, but below whites. The mulatto woman was perceived as, and perceived herself to be, more beautiful than the black woman, and she was more acceptable to the dominant white ruling class.

Although appearances and common official claims may suggest the contrary, a radical change in racial perceptions has not accompanied the improvements in the legal and social status of Afro-Caribbean people in postcolonial times. Such an uneven development dates back to the early nationalist rhetoric of the nineteenth-century movements for political independence. José Martí, for example, widely regarded as the most outstanding exponent of Cuban nationalism in the period, emphasized unconditional equality for all, but still perceived the Negro as uncivilized and culturally inferior (Mansour, 108–9). In postrevolution Cuba the privileging of class over race has led to the official posture that the socialist order has eliminated the problem of discrimination against blacks. Yet in Cuba, and in the rest of the Caribbean, appearance (skin color and other physical features) persists as a strong basis of prejudice. In slave society the black woman was the most subordinate woman and was perceived as the least attractive. In postcolonial society she still occupies the lowest place on the scale of aesthetic values.

Race and color are, in one sense, theoretical abstractions, constructs of ideology. They also influence the lived experience of many Caribbean people. Vestiges of the original white racial bias persist today in the construction of light skin and "white" (Caucasian) features as the ideal of female beauty. Caribbean racial politics therefore excludes many Negroid women, who, because they also subscribe to the alien ideal, fail to develop positive self images. Sporadic attempts have been made to counter this bias. In 1965, three years after the declaration of Jamaica's political independence, the Council for Afro-Jamaican Affairs noted that the "racial balance of contestants in the Miss Jamaica beauty competitions has been weighted against the majority of the population." The Council recommended that to correct this imbalance, the contest should be exclusively for "black girls" for the next three years (1966–1968), and in 1969 for minority groups (qtd. in *Jamaican Daily Gleaner*, Sept. 12, 1996, p. 5B). But the recalcitrance of racism has largely aborted such efforts to erase the stigmatization of black women. It is this residue of colonial ideology that has been the most difficult to eradicate and that has offered the greatest resistance to the movement for decolonization. Literary practice in the Caribbean has functioned in some instances to advance and in others to retard this process.

The historical context outlined above is necessary for an adequate understanding of the racial images of the woman of African descent that Caribbean writers have created. Caribbean literature has not only participated in the process that has reaffirmed and disseminated racial attitudes, but has itself contributed to the formation of these attitudes. In the movement to change racial perception, literature has performed the important function of creating new images to displace the conventional stereotypes. Spanish Caribbean literature, almost from the moment of its inception, has made the racial dynamic one of its central concerns. However, overt aesthetic disparagement of the woman of African extraction is a purpose this literature has rarely served. Although the Afro-Caribbean woman's color is seldom evoked with deprecatory intent, the effects of this representational practice are sometimes less than favorable.

Preoccupation with the physical characteristics of the Negro is especially prominent among Spanish Caribbean writers and, as Lemuel Johnson has observed, is dominant in the Hispanic literary tradition in general (*Devil*, 68). Although not always specified, the racial identity of the women who inspire these writers is specified frequently enough to indicate the extent to which race consciousness informs creative writing. Race is most frequently perceived as a physical category, and color labels are rarely neutral; writers invest explicit or implied aesthetic value in the visual imagery of their literary portrayals. Not all the physical depictions of the Afro-Caribbean woman imply aesthetic judgment, but some seemingly innocuous portrayals conceal deeply rooted, though involuntary, prejudice. At the same time, a study of the construction of race in Spanish

Caribbean societies needs to take into account the fluid value of certain racial terms. Epithets such as "negra" and "prieta" (dark) indicate Negroid characteristics, but are also used as expressions of affection without racial connotations, even between individuals with no black racial heritage. Another tendency that is very evident in social intercourse is the preference for polite variants such as "morena" (brown) and "trigueña" (wheat-colored), which are used to avoid the overtones of racial insult acquired by "black" and "Negro."

Colonial Caribbean writers were the heirs to a European literary and artistic tradition in which aesthetic devaluation and racial disparagement of the Negro were the standard practice. In the introduction to her 1987 anthology Ann Venture Young cites many examples of early metropolitan Spanish writers who constituted black as the aesthetic opposite of white (the ideal of beauty). They also established a strict correspondence between the moral character and the perceived aesthetic value of the Negro. For them the Negro came to signify the embodiment of evil. Caricature and other burlesque modes were the literary modalities used almost perennially for the portrayal of blacks by these writers. Their representations of the black woman bear the signs of this tradition. One can hardly refer to her frequent appearance in this early literature without adding that the writers usually depicted her as a creature without validity and as an aesthetic and moral foil for the white woman. From as early as the tenth century, the written literature represented female beauty as white and the black woman as ugly. In popular poetry too, the black woman served as the necessary antithesis of the white woman's beauty and virtue. Despite intermittent efforts at aesthetic redemption, the disparagement of the nonwhite woman persisted in the written tradition of metropolitan Spanish literature up to the nineteenth century. This practice depended upon the polarization of racial groups in that society. In the colonies, however, the unfixing of the racial poles (symbolized by the rise of the mulatto class) motivated a shift in representational practice.

Rehabilitation of the Afro-Caribbean woman's aesthetic image in Caribbean literature has arisen mainly in the context of nationalism, which was born in Haiti early in the nineteenth century and between the turn of the century and the 1940s in the other territories. During this period writers, particularly those from Haiti and the English-speaking territories, have been deliberately transgressive in their portrayals as they reject European standards of beauty. This motive, though not without ambiguity, has also inspired some Spanish Caribbean writers.

Nineteenth-century writers showed their submission to the inherited European tradition both in their vision and in their expression. Romantic idealization of literary subjects was typical of the period, and a wide breach separated the literary fantasies of these early writers from colonial reality. Society's perception of the Negroid woman as unattractive is nowhere evident in the ode "The Sable Venus," written by the Reverend Isaac Teale and included by his friend Bryan Edwards in his 1801 *History of the British Colonies in the West Indies:*

> Her skin excelled the raven plume,
> Her breath the fragrant orange bloom,
> Her eye the tropick beam:
> Soft was her lip as silken down,
> And mild her look as ev'ning sun
> That gilds the COBRE stream.
> The loveliest limbs her form compose,
> Such as her sister VENUS chose,
> In FLORENCE, where she's seen;
> Both just alike, except the white,
> No difference, no—none at night,
> The beauteous dames between. (Edwards, 35)

In the view of Edwards, this poem illustrates "the character of the sable and saffron beauties of the West-Indies and the folly of their paramours" (31). Although he claims realism for Teale's portrait, it is obviously the creation of a mythifying Romantic imagination. The speaker superimposes the European-derived discourse on the Caribbean subject, with the result that he falsifies reality and causes her to lose her specific identity.

Ostensibly, the poem's motive is to erase the perception of aesthetic difference between white and dark-skinned women ("The loveliest limbs her form compose, / Such as her sister VENUS chose, / In FLORENCE, where she's seen"). However, this is deliberately aborted by a skillful sleight of hand that retracts the earlier statement: "No difference, *no—none at night*, / The beauteous dames between" (my emphasis), and by the ode's final stanza:

> Should then the song too wanton seem,
> You know who chose th' unlucky theme,
> Dear Bryan tell the truth. (38)

The speaker is clearly engaging in an act of insincere poetizing, in a whimsical rather than an earnest attempt at aesthetic vindication of the Afro-Caribbean woman.

In Haiti, despite the rise of a nationalist movement in the early post-emancipation years, the inherited French colonial tradition hampered the attempt to create new literary models. Often, the women whose beauty the poets celebrated were hardly recognizable as Haitian or black. The poets (mainly mulatto) who wrote about them were the products of colonial culture and were still too steeped in it to find a voice and a vision of their own. Some, however, had already begun to express an unequivocal appreciation for the beauty of the Negroid woman. In one instance the poet sees the beauty of the woman on a slave ship:

> She was at the prow; you would swear you were seeing
> So beautiful, with tears flowing on her cheek,
> The angel that comes in our even-time dreams.
>   (qtd. in Hoffmann, 90)

In this poem the tendency toward romanticizing lingers in the transformation of the slave into an angel. But the perfunctory mention of tears flowing on her cheeks makes it evident that fascination with her beauty blinds the speaker to the pain of her enslavement. As early as 1842 Haitian poet Pierre Faubert, though writing in the Romantic tradition, expressed unashamed love for the black woman's color in the poem "The Negress" (La Négresse):

> I am proud to say it, O Black woman, I love you
> And I like your black color, and do you know why?
> Because Heaven endowed you with noble virtues,
> A chaste heart, beauty even, in short, all that is charming.
>   (qtd. in Hoffmann, 93)

Affirmation is undeniably the main impulse of this poem, as is the poet's consciousness of doing the untoward in declaring his love for the black woman. Looked at with some scruple, however, this celebration appears reluctant. The poet's investment in the black woman's color is primarily moral ("noble virtues" and "chaste heart") and only belatedly aesthetic ("beauty even"). Physical beauty was not readily admitted in the black woman. Similar ambiguities characterize nineteenth-century Cuban portrayals of the *mulata*.

The Beautiful *Mulata* and the Invisible Black Woman

Cuba produced one of the earliest stereotypes of the woman of African descent in Caribbean literature. The beautiful *mulata* image recurs in antislavery narrative and in the oral and written poetry of the nineteenth century. At that time many poets showed a veritable obsession with the *mulata*. Both transgression and orthodoxy were inherent in the construction of this stereotype. The ideological impulse was subversive; poets made a deliberate effort to rehabilitate the image of the nonwhite woman, whose aesthetic value had been depreciated by white ethnocentrism. The aesthetic method, however, was orthodox, as writers adopted the ready-made European Romantic mode of expression to celebrate her beauty.

In the folk tradition there is a displacement of the European discourse of color. Although this poetry identifies the woman racially as not white, color itself is not the focus of the image-making process. Through a substitution of icons, the idealized white woman of European poetry is replaced by an equally idealized *mulata,* viewed through the eyes of a male lover. The language of these compositions manifests a Romantic consciousness, as the following poems illustrate:

> The eyes of my mulatto girl
> are the stars of her soul.
> My heart is inspired
> by the glow from their sparks. (qtd. in Arrom, "Presencia," 130)

> She is the prettiest mulatto girl
> born in el Manglar.
> I will always follow her,
> Love her I always will. (qtd. in Arrom, "Presencia," 130)

A transposition of the Romantic spirit is also evident in the written poetry of the nineteenth century. Two poems about local women, by the most well known Afro-Cuban poets who wrote during slavery, exemplify different ideological uses of the inherited Romantic convention. In the early nineteenth century the black slave poet Juan Francisco Manzano writes "Ilusiones," a poem about the pain of his impossible love for the beautiful and inaccessible lady:

> Her tender, youthful, beautiful brow
> like a gleaming poppy, her hair
> of shiny perfumed ebony;

her cheeks of roses and violets,
her black eyes and purple lips,
the dainty air of her graceful form
that showed no lust in its movement;
in a corner of Cuba to me was shown
a divine being in human form. (qtd. in Guirao, 24–25)

Certain signs are noteworthy in this poem. In the first place, Manzano provides us with no clue that would help to place his female subject racially. In the face of this absence, the "cheeks of roses and violets," the shiny (rather than curly) hair, and the Romantic body carefully divested of all sensuality might even create the impression that it is a white woman who embodies ideal beauty for the poet. However, in the final stanza the woman is named as Delia (presumed to be Manzano's mulatto wife). His denial of her sensuality demonstrates that Manzano is a slave to the white racist notion that the nonwhite woman's sensuality is a sign of lasciviousness.

Like Manzano, the free mulatto poet Plácido (Gabriel de la Concepción Valdés, 1809–1844) appropriates the language of Romantic idealization, using it explicitly to celebrate the beauty of a "brown girl":

the light of dawn,
whose glow the birds praise
with their song,
is not as beautiful,
as my brown girl's eyes. (qtd. in Morales, 308)

Although Plácido wrote this poem about a mulatto woman named Fela, except for the use of "morena" to indicate her skin color, the poem does not center on the woman's distinguishing racial features. Instead, the speaker concentrates his imaginative energy on giving standard Romantic contours to her image. The language of his portrait is similar to the language of Manzano's poem, but the racial specificity of Plácido's representation diminishes the former's ambiguity.

In another poem, "Sugar Cane Blossom" (La flor de la caña), Plácido uses Romantic discourse to paint a picture of the dark-skinned woman:

I saw a country girl
wheat-colored, and tanned
. . . .
Her voice, divine,
Her bright-red lips

> Her graceful body,
> Her light feet,
> And the blond tresses
> that float at the whim
> of the zephyr wind, shine
> brightly with pearly ornaments;
> Like the sugar cane blossom
> shines brightly with
> the dewdrops of the dawn. (qtd. in Stimson, 36–37)

Plácido's subject might easily have been a white woman. All the imagery, except the color epithets "wheat-colored" and "tanned," denotes the stereotype of the ideal white female body: red lips, blond tresses, and slender figure. Expressions such as these lend validity to the claim that Plácido is an example of an Afro-Caribbean writer whose imitation of the writing of the dominant white culture is symptomatic of the self-denying mentality of the colonized.

This is a cultural phenomenon that can be more fully appreciated when it is placed in its historical context. The absence of an unequivocal black consciousness in an Afro-Caribbean poet, such as Plácido, is a function of his historical location. Plácido wrote in the context of a still-segregated society, where blacks were the most marginalized group, and where mulattoes not only sought to align themselves with the white ruling class but were more acceptable to that class. These relations of race and power would have exercised a significant influence on the literary posture of such non-white writers, who depended on the consumption (and, in the case of Manzano, on the patronage) of the ruling class. In fact, they would no doubt have been denied access to the means of publication had their work been perceived as a challenge to white supremacy. They were therefore limited to writing in the manner and about the subjects that the established order permitted. Plácido's whitening of the *mulata* is perhaps less an indication of his acceptance of white aesthetic norms than it is a reflection of the state of cultural politics in colonial Cuban society.

When compared with later and more vigorous attempts at aesthetic vindication, these poets' efforts appear feeble. But one needs to bear in mind that they wrote at a time when Eurocentrism had not yet been seriously challenged. Their deliberate choice of poetic subject is, therefore, a politically significant act, given the hegemony of white female beauty in the prevailing system of aesthetic values. In spite of the euphemism of the racial references, these were the first recognized poets in colonial Cuba who not only saw beauty in the dark-skinned woman but deemed it fit for celebration in lyrical verse. They wrote about her beauty without the benefit of an inherited tradition. Their poems mark the first stage of the development of a subversive aesthetic practice in Caribbean literature, the beginning of the gradual liberation of the aesthetic discourse from the thralldom of European norms. Although it is Romantic ideology that determines the form of expression, a new idea (appreciation of the beauty of the *mulata*) has been introduced into the poetic discourse.

A first step toward the Caribbeanization of the literary process was to find a language to depict local reality. Plácido recognized the dissonance between the discourse inherited from Europe and the distinctiveness of the local subject matter. Poems such as "Sugar Cane Blossom" may be taken as a sign of the emergence of such a Caribbeanized discourse. By incorporating vocabulary and imagery from the local environment, the poet has modified the Romantic mode, thus giving literary expression to what Gordon K. Lewis has described as an "early spirit of colonial assertion" (69). The sugar cane blossom is an appropriately Caribbean metaphor for the *mulata*'s beauty. This attempt to correlate aesthetic discourse and nationalist ideology is a practice later writers were to follow more rigorously in their quest for culturally distinct female icons.

White Cuban writers of the nineteenth century also showed their fascination with the *mulata*'s racial character. They created a more complex racial image, highlighting her physical appearance, color, culture, and moral character. Their depictions reflected her difference (her nonwhiteness) and her refusal to be contained in the conventional Romantic mold. These writers perceived the need to redefine the *mulata*'s beauty as sensual to distinguish it from pure white female beauty. Their ambivalence leads to the suspicion that this distinction was also tainted with residual racial prejudice. In "La mulata," a poem published in 1845, color difference is the basis on which Francisco Muñoz del Monte, a Dominican poet living in Cuba, constructs his image of the *mulata*. His portrait preserves the binary opposition of white and nonwhite and affirms (albeit obliquely) the dominance of the white aesthetic ideal:

You are not white, *mulata*,
your hair is not pure gold,
your neck is not like silver,
your eyes do not mirror

the sky's heavenly blue.
But your fiery eye
burns like Vesuvius,
and drop by drop you feel
the flame of love
run down your burning cheek.
And beneath your purple lip
your teeth their whiteness show,
like pure snow
lying in the cold crater
of a red-hot volcano. (qtd. in Morales, 197)

Being unable to define the *mulata's* beauty in intrinsic terms, the poet defines it as lack of whiteness. In this way, unwittingly perhaps, he has left unchallenged the authority of the ideology that has idolized the blue-eyed blond. By strategically placing the words "you are not white" at the beginning of his description, he reminds the *mulata* of her racial and, by extension, social inferiority. In other words, the poet has transposed into this piece the desire of the white ruling class to keep the mulatto class in its place. However, the ostensible main purpose of the poem has veiled this agenda.

Counterbalancing his initial representation of the *mulata's* difference as absence—deviation from the white aesthetic ideal—is his affirmation of her sensuality. A shift from visual (golden hair, silver neck, and sky-blue eyes) to tactile imagery (burning pupils, red-hot cheeks, mouth like the seething crater of a volcano) marks the distinction between the white woman's aesthetic appeal and the *mulata's* sensual endowment. Yet certain anomalies inhere in this representation. Although the poet has drawn on a literary convention that has idealized woman as the fair sex, the *mulata's* beauty is distinct not only in its sensuality but more importantly because it is the beauty of the proverbial evil woman. To amplify this perspective, elsewhere in the poem the speaker carefully likens his subject to icons from the Judeo-Christian and Greco-Roman traditions—Eve, Circe, Helen of Troy. These figures stand as symbols of that kind of beauty that seduces in order to destroy. In the final analysis, the unfavorable connotations of this imagery undermine any intended validation.

That this definition of the beauty of the *mulata* as sensual but deadly was well entrenched in the Cuban mind is also evident in the folk poetry of the period:

Here is the mulatto girl
the sweetest and most alluring girl
in all Havana,
and her gaze is deadly. (qtd. in Arrom, "Presencia," 130)

With this representational method, these poets were repudiating Euro-centric standards and creating their own local aesthetic models. Their in-corporation of the *mulata* as a poetic figure might be taken as an index of the liberalization of racial attitudes in nineteenth-century Cuba and of a rapprochement between nonwhites and whites.

While the poets celebrated the *mulata*, however, there was an aversive element in their response to the black woman. She was conspicuous by her lack of representation in this poetry. Even this rare poem, "Colors" (Colores), written in 1878 by Diego Vicente Tejera and featuring the black slave woman, makes use of a strategy of evasion:

How white is the lady!
How black her poor slave!
But, if the colors of their souls
should show on their faces
How white would be the black woman!
How black would be the white! (qtd. in Mansour, 125)

Tejera inscribes not an aesthetic but a moral value on the woman's black-ness. He has inverted the color symbolism of Christian morality that has constructed good as white and evil as black. But his inversion is aborted because it fails to overturn the conventional moral scale of values connoted by *black* and *white*. Before it can be cast as virtuous, the soul of the black slave must first be cast as white. Thus, in the eyes of this nineteenth-century poet, the black woman is unrepresentable in positive aesthetic terms. Her appearance in the novel, with its more panoramic scope and its use of slave characters, hardly changed this picture.

Nineteenth-century Cuban narrative gives a more nuanced picture of the racial politics of the period. The producers of the so-called antislavery novels reflect the general anxiety in colonial Cuba to define characters in racial and aesthetic terms. Black and mulatto female characters played important and minor roles in these novels, but as Sharon Fivel-Démoret cogently illustrates in "La belle ou la bête," the discrimination in their treatment is as flagrant as the difference between Beauty and the Beast. The mulatto slaves Camila in Antonio Zambrana's *El negro Francisco*

(1873) and Dorotea in Anselmo Suárez y Romero's *Francisco* (1880), for example, are portrayed as creatures of extraordinary beauty. But unlike the poets, who expressed their prejudice more subtly by excluding the black woman, the novelists were frequently blatant in degrading her physical appearance as ugly. Both Conchón and Josefa Lucumí in Francisco Calcagno's *Romualdo: Uno de tantos* fall into this latter category.

But in none of these novels is the Cuban fascination with the *mulata* as conspicuous as in *Cecilia Valdés*, written by Cirilo Villaverde between 1839 and 1882. One of this author's primary representational techniques is fastidiously detailed physical character description heavily laden with racial signs and aesthetic appraisals. Although Villaverde acknowledges strength as a positive attribute in some of his black female characters, he is generally loath to ascribe beauty to them. On the other hand, the author describes the beauty of Cecilia, the mulatto protagonist, at length and in hyperbolically Romantic terms: "[She was] perhaps the woman with the most beautiful face living in Havana during that period" (I:228); "Well could she have passed for the Venus of the hybrid African-Caucasian race" (I:142). Both the narrator and the other characters worship her because of her phenomenal beauty: "All the women turned to look at her, the men made way for her, threw her a compliment, and in a moment a quiet murmur ran from one end of the dance hall to the other: The *Bronze Virgin*, the *Bronze Virgin*" (I:142). In a novel in which the realist narrative mode predominates and the narrator constantly reminds the reader of the veracity of his tale, Cecilia is nevertheless presented as a Romantically conceived myth. Villaverde's representation of his protagonist differs from that of other *mulatas* in the novel only in degree. Cecilia's mulatto grandmother, Josefa, conforms to the stereotype: "In spite of her mature years and her suffering, she still maintained the signs of a beautiful and distinguished youth, pretty eyes, an amorously expressive mouth, round neck, shoulders and arms" (I:96).

Hortensia Ruiz del Vizo offers a favorable assessment of Villaverde's stereotype, claiming that the novel established the *mulata* as the ideal of female beauty in Cuba (*Poesía*, 13). But the patently rhapsodic praise of the *mulata*'s beauty in Villaverde's novel is not as unproblematic as Ruiz del Vizo's assertion suggests. In fact, the narrator's praise is so extreme in its exuberance that it becomes suspect, given the contrasting reality of race relations in Cuban slave society. The novel's celebration of Cecilia's beauty obscures but does not obliterate the prevailing racial prejudice against mulattoes.

Although the narrator sustains his rhapsody for most of the novel, at some points he introduces surreptitiously the then-current racist thesis about the mulatto's inferiority. The novel contains various signs of ambivalence, of ostensible admiration masking real contempt for what the *mulata* represents racially: "When one recalls her careless upbringing and adds to it the obscene compliments paid her by men, precisely because she was of a hybrid and inferior race, one will have a general idea of her pride and vanity, the secret motives of her imperious character. Thus, shamelessly and without hesitation she often displayed her preference for men of the superior white race" (I:153–54). With such obtrusive comments the author effectively subverts the so-called cult of the *mulata* in nineteenth-century Cuba. Villaverde's account contains no hint of opposition to this racist idea. Cecilia's extraordinary beauty is not sufficient to allow her to transcend her inferior status. She is, in the final analysis, a presumptuous *mulata* who has dared to aspire to social advancement through affiliation with a white man.

A similar racist sentiment underlies the portrayal of Cecilia's mulatto mother: "Oval face, as pale as wax . . . a sharp chin, high, square brow, small mouth, thick lips, a well-formed nose *for a woman of mixed race.* . . . The complete picture was beautiful, feminine" (I:98, my emphasis). Most telling in this affirmation of beauty are the qualifying words in italics, which signal complicity with the idea of white racial superiority. These words establish that the *mulata's* beauty is an anomaly and, by extension, that beauty resides naturally in the racially pure (white) woman.

Black female characters, with their clearly visible racial difference, do not detain Villaverde's narrator, as his summary treatment of his Negroid women characters illustrates: "a squalid old Negress, the very image of death" (I:97). In some instances his description of these women makes no aesthetic judgment; one tortilla vendor is "fat and heavy," and another is round like the tortillas she sells (I:226). Villaverde is not indisposed to acknowledge, albeit in a perfunctory manner, beauty in black slave women. Dolores is "young, well shaped and pretty for a black woman" (I:410), and the runaway Tomasa is "young, robust and attractive" (II:173). But he subjects the *mulata*, whose African ancestry was frequently not so visible, to maniacal scrutiny to establish her exact racial pedigree. Even the shape of a face is a telltale sign: "She had a sallow complexion resulting from the mixture of a black female and an Indian male. But her curly hair and oval face admitted not the probability of such a mixture but the mixture of a black mother and a white father" (I:96).

At the heart of Villaverde's fixation with the *mulata* is his anxiety to safeguard white racial purity. He places meticulous emphasis on the physical traits that betray the nonwhiteness of his near-white *mulatas*—curly hair, full lips, and less-than-white skin: "Her complexion could be considered healthy . . . , although looking carefully one could notice that though ruddy, the color of her face had too much of a brownish tint and was neither clear nor smooth. To what race, then, did this girl belong? It is difficult to say. However, what could not escape a knowing eye was the fact that her red lips had a dark border or edge, and that the glow of her face ended with a kind of shadow toward the hairline. Her blood was not pure and it was certain that back in the third or fourth generation it had mixed with African blood" (I:105). Villaverde's "knowing eye" is the eye of the vigilant white Cuban, anxious to preserve the fast-disappearing purity of his race and to ward off the danger that mulattoes (and especially mulatto women) posed for white supremacy.

In addition, evil tarnishes Cecilia's sensual beauty: "Her mouth was small, her lips full, suggesting more voluptuousness than firmness of character. Her full round cheeks and the dimple in the center of her chin formed a beautiful picture, which would have been perfect if it had been less roguish, if not evil" (I:105). The *mulata's* irresistible beauty is inseparable from its dangerous potential.

Writing about mulatto women in the colonial period was a sign of the birth of local consciousness, the embryonic stage of the move to break the cultural hegemony of Europe. Although the writers were conscious of and heavily dependent on European models and conventions, the difference of the woman of African descent had started to impose itself. Literary interest in the *mulata* illustrates how the unfixing of the racial poles in this period served to mitigate the racial disparagement of nonwhites popularized in the preceding European artistic tradition. At the same time, the writers' discrimination between black and mulatto women shows the literary reproduction of the race and power relations of nineteenth-century Cuban society. Their preference for the *mulata* suggests that the dominant white Europeans recognized the futility of ignoring the increasingly more visible mixed group. Even while they were anxious to ensure that its members remained in their assigned place in the socio-racial hierarchy, they were beginning to draw them into the social mainstream. Exclusion or disparagement of black women, on the other hand, is the hidden side of this development.

Out of the Literary Wilderness: Redeeming the Black Woman

With the intensification of the decolonization movement in the early twentieth century, Spanish Caribbean writers began to promote the black woman, as distinct from the *mulata*, as a literary icon. Encouraged by the interest in the Negro since the late 1920s, and the spirit of cultural nationalism that generated it, many writers have sought to invest her physical features with positive aesthetic value and to propagate the notion that beauty may reside in blackness.

During the years immediately preceding the *negrista* movement, writers in Cuba and Puerto Rico made sporadic moves toward aesthetic rehabilitation of the black woman. One of the earliest attempts is found in the poem "Black Woman" (La negra), published by Luis Lloréns Torres of Puerto Rico in 1914. He applies the prevailing literary mode to an unfamiliar subject:

> Beneath evening's shady canopy,
> the hand of Jehovah, filled with an excess
> of the Biblical light of the all-shining fiat,
> molded you from the rough skin of the serpent.
>
> He put in your skin the dye of Moroccan leather
> and in your teeth the foam of coconut milk.
> Your breasts he gave the magic of a mountain spring
> and your thighs the texture of polished mahogany.
>
> Madonna, when your flesh trembles in your hips,
> you are like the filly pawing the meadow.
> Mother, the divine stream flowing from your bosom,
>
> runs like a shining number on a slate.
> Oh, you who are worthy of him who was drunk with inspiration,
> song of songs of King Solomon. (qtd. in Morales, 41)

Concern with pictorial and exotic effect and with creating elegant beauty are the imperatives that determine the attitude of the speaker in this poem. His idealization of the black woman is consistent with the then-dominant *modernista* poetic practice and its penchant for refinement. Appropriately exotic and sensory imagery is used to celebrate the woman's beauty—from her snakeskin body to her Moroccan-leather complexion and coconut-milky white teeth. Allusions to the biblical creation story and the analogy with the Queen of Sheba, whose beauty is exalted in the Song of Solomon, further mythify the image. Modernist *preciosismo* is also evident in the elegant metaphors used to avoid the banality of the literal reference to her breasts and thighs.

But the mythical tone that marks the first two stanzas of this sonnet, a form that has been used traditionally to pay homage to woman, is not sustained. In the second half of the poem, the focus shifts to the more mundane aspects of the woman's identity. On the one hand, the inclusion of her sexuality and maternal function adds a human dimension to the preceding abstract image. On the other, the first of the two tercets introduces an ambivalent note, where the nonsexual expectations raised by the title "Madonna" (virgin) conflict with the contiguous sexualized image of the panting filly. Such a contradiction is another indication of the resistance encountered in these attempts to find perfect accommodation for a purely aesthetic image of the black woman within the established literary conventions. As we will see in the next chapter, poets of the next two decades appropriated this sexual image and consolidated it into a stereotype.

Lloréns Torres's poem represents a unique contribution to the iconography of the black woman in Puerto Rican poetry, where it is the *mulata* who is the more frequently evoked icon of nonwhite beauty. Placed within the context of the collection in which it appears, and the poetic creed on which it is based, its radical import becomes more apparent. In the preface to the collection (*Sonetos sinfónicos*), the poet states that the cultivation of beauty is the highest good, and that "the poet's mission is not to sing the beauty that we all see, but to show us the beauty that our eyes will not or cannot see" (93). This last assertion seems especially relevant to the effect of this piece. At the time of its composition in 1914, more than a decade before the consolidation of the movement to vindicate blacks and their culture, Lloréns Torres perceives and glorifies the black woman's intrinsic beauty. But although he achieves this without reference to white aesthetic standards, he has shaped her image as an abstraction without any suggestion of her Caribbean particularity.

Alfonso Camín, an Asturian poet who spent most of his adult life in Cuba, is more successful in his attempt to create a distinctive image of the Caribbean black woman. He wrote his "Tribute to the Black Woman" (Elogio de la negra) in 1925:

Black woman with thick sensual lips;
your eyes, wide like the mysteries of the night,

Black woman, your teeth
so fresh and fleshy like the water coconut,
and your silky dark skin
like the cigar leaves of Cumanayagua;
Your mouth like brown sugar,
thick and dark like Cuban love. (qtd. in Ruiz del Vizo, *Poesía*, 26)

Camín's frank celebration of the woman's Negroid features includes imagery that allows her to retain her Cuban identity. Unlike Lloréns Torres's choice of exotic allusions, this poem creates analogies between the woman and objects specific to Cuban reality. Both poems, however, despite the divergence in their imagery, express the will to break the stranglehold of the dominant white aesthetic ideal and to counteract antiblack prejudice.

In contrast to these earlier occasional efforts, in the decade of the 1930s Afro-Cuban poet Nicolás Guillén undertakes a sustained program of aesthetic redemption of the black woman. In the first of the two poems entitled "Madrigal" from his 1931 collection, *Sóngoro cosongo*, Guillén develops his physical portrait in a style that is more sober and less elaborate than the celebration of Camín:

From your hands
your nails drip
like a bunch of ten purple grapes.
Your skin,
heart of a scorched tree trunk,
which runs aground in the glassy waters
and smokes the timid algae. (*Obra poética*, I:121)

In both the sentiment and the form of this poem, Guillén is writing within the bounds of European convention. But his incorporation of the woman's black color into the poetic discourse solely for its visual, pictorial effect suggests a view of her racial characteristics as having intrinsic aesthetic value.

Other poems in the collection show signs of an emerging Africa-centered discourse as a new mode for paying homage to the black woman. When he gave the very explicit title "New Woman" (Mujer nueva) to another of these poems, Guillén signaled his choice of a fresh rhetorical strategy:

With the circle of the equator
girded on her waist as if on a small globe,

the black woman, a new woman,
advances in her sheer serpent's robe.
Crowned with palm leaves
like a newly arrived goddess,
she brings the new word,
strong loins,
her voice, teeth, the morning and the leap forward. (*Obra poética*,
    I:120–21)

One of the categories that Edward Brathwaite has identified in his study of the African influence in Caribbean literature is the "literature of African reconnection." In this type of work, the writer makes a conscious attempt to link the New World to Africa by seeking "meaningful correlates" from Africa to transform Afro-Caribbean reality ("African," 100). With this poem, Guillén achieves a subtle Africanization of the black woman's poetic image. He has appropriated a conventional metaphor that identifies woman with the earth, but the specific geographical landscape with which he associates her is that of the African continent. His vision of the black woman as a continuation of Africa in the New World serves effectively to displace the dominant Eurocentric aesthetic discourse that focuses on color.

Guillén continues the Africa-centered trend in the second "Madrigal," where he uses the classical poetic form but weaves African motifs into the imagery:

Your belly knows more than your head
and as much as your thighs.
That
is the strong black grace
of your naked body.
Yours is the sign of the jungle
with your red necklaces
your bracelets of curved gold,
and that dark alligator
swimming in your Zambezi eyes. (*Obra poética*, I:121–22)

Though rhetorical and romantic, this evocation of Africa does not merely add an exotic touch to his representation of the woman. It is an attempt to construct her physical identity in terms of its continuity with her African origins. While the poem repeats the stereotype of the instinct-dominated

Negro ("Your belly knows more than your head"), the casting of her eyes as the Zambezi river in the final line is an adept blending of African imagery and the African landscape into the aesthetic discourse.

Another feature of Guillén's Africa-oriented discourse of racial aesthetics is the recurring references to the black woman's physical strength. Nineteenth-century Cuban narrative had grounded such an attribution upon the widely accepted notion of her inordinate capacity to withstand the hard physical labor and brutal punishment of slavery. In "Madrigal," as in "Mujer Nueva," Guillén ascribes beauty to the physical strength of her body. Strength is also a dominant feature in Haitian writers' configuration of the black woman's beauty. Twentieth-century Haitian novelists have highlighted this attribute in their black working-class female characters with remarkable frequency (see Latortue 65–69).

This Africa-centered focus in Guillén's poetry beginning in the 1930s is part of a movement in the Americas to challenge the hegemony of European ideology, to counter the depreciation of things African, and to diffuse positive images of people of African descent. At this point Guillén's poetry converges with the ethos of French Caribbean *négritude* of the 1940s. In "Black Beauty" (1943), Guy Tirolien of Guadeloupe promotes a similar Africanist aesthetic image of the Negroid woman:

> your breasts of black satin
> trembling to the gallop of your blood
> leaping
> your arms supple and long rippling in their sleekness
> that white smile
> eyes
> set in a night-sky face
> waken in me
> this night
> the muffled rhythms
> the clapping hands
> the slow and measured chantings
> that over in the land of Guinea intoxicate
> our sisters
> black and bare
> and bring forth in me
> this night
> dark-skinned twilights heavy with passion

for the soul of the black land where ancients sleep
lives and speaks this night
in the sweep of restless strength along your loins
in the languorous leisure of a proud unhurried pace
that leaves
in your wake
as you pass
the wild allure of nights expanded
and pervaded
by the immense pulsation of the fevered

tom-

toms.

(qtd. in Shapiro, 65)

Tirolien validates the sensual beauty of the black woman intrinsically and not against white standards. He does not present her sensuality as compensation for her lack of whiteness, nor does he achieve his vindication through objectification of the woman. The speaker has positioned himself clearly within her world, so that, beyond the erotic interest she holds, she is united with him in a deeper spiritual bond deriving from their common link with an African past. As in Guillén's "New Woman," the Africa-centered frame of this poet's vision represents an important milestone in the journey of Caribbean poets toward liberation from alienating Euro-centric aesthetic models. For them, it was Africa that could provide the most appropriate context for the aesthetic characterization of the black woman.

Meanwhile, a strengthening nationalism began to produce celebrations of the Afro-Caribbean woman's beauty in the colonial romantic mode in English-speaking Caribbean literature of the 1940s. One of the earliest examples is Jamaican poet George Campbell's 1945 portrait of the mulatto woman in "O Solomon's fair." Like Lloréns Torres, Campbell links her beauty to her procreative capacity:

O woven of the night
This beauty of her race
O garden is her hair;
Dawnlight in her eyes
Forgotten surmise
Adam has sown.
O glorious peak

Procreative power
The woman Eve
Twix dark and light
O Solomon's fair
O shadowed flower! (35)

In the year that Jamaica gained political independence (1962), Edward Baugh used understatement in "There's a Brown Girl in the Ring" to achieve an end similar to Guillén's:

When I speak of this woman I do not mean
To indicate the Muse or abstract queen
But to record the brown fact of her being,
The undiluted blackness of her hair
And that I lightly kissed her knee
And how her feet were shy before my stare. (qtd. in Morris, 24)

Here the intention is to convey unaffected racial assertion through bald statement rather than literary pose. The speaker personalizes his portrait and deliberately opposes the bare "brown fact" of her being to that kind of mythification of the Afro-Caribbean woman practiced by early nationalist poets such as Campbell. Baugh's persona can relate to his "brown girl" as a flesh-and-blood woman, as part of an everyday reality.

Despite the preceding instances of revolt, white aesthetic standards have persisted in the postcolonial era, as the center from which some Spanish Caribbean writers measure the physical features of the Afro-Caribbean woman. They have continued to cast her as a figure of racial deviance. "Mulatto Girl" (La mulata), written by Cuban poet Gustavo Sánchez-Galarraga most probably between 1920 and 1934, exemplifies the phenomenon. The male speaker invokes the *mulata* in an apparent move to decenter white female beauty:

She is not blessed with whiteness
and her brown color betrays her;
but, what does color matter
when sweetness oozes from her hips?
Her tempting eyes burn
with the fires of lust,
and her erotic body sways,
and writhes like a serpent. (qtd. in Ruiz del Vizo, "*Poesía,* 34)

This poem belongs to the period of heightened nationalist sensibility and preoccupation with defining a Caribbean identity. The poet expresses this spirit by using the white woman, who is celebrated for her pure beauty, unsullied by sexuality, as a foil for the *mulata*. First he establishes the aesthetic ideal to which the *mulata* is allegedly inferior. He refers ironically to the prevailing understanding of whiteness as a desirable characteristic and dark skin as a defect in the statement "and her brown color betrays her." In posing the subsequent rhetorical question to brush aside her color as unimportant, the poet intends to refute this negative perception. But his strategy is tantamount to evasion, for its effect is to leave unchallenged and even to perpetuate the ideology of white aesthetic superiority.

The rest of the poem, ostensibly a vindication of the *mulata*, appreciates an alternate attribute that she is deemed to possess—her body's powerful sensuality. But the achievement of that aim is vitiated, perhaps unintentionally, by the strategy used. Rather than contest the popular perception, the speaker merely suggests that the *mulata*'s sexual appeal compensates for her aesthetic deficiency. The poet is evidently consciously introducing the sensual image to counter the discourse that had sanctioned the celebration of "pure" female beauty. In the end, however, his attempted redemption of the *mulata* is partially aborted. For, while the speaker succeeds in boosting the image of her sensual vitality, he has also demonstrated implicit acceptance of the notion that there is an aesthetic ideal from which she deviates.

Other Caribbean writers of the period have also been reluctant or unable to express unqualified appreciation of the black woman's beauty. Such an ambivalence lies at the center of the presumably well intentioned attempt by Haitian poet Philippe Thoby-Marcellin to sing the praises of the Negroid woman in "Little Black Girl" (Petite noire), written in 1926:

> Thick lips, flat nose, she is really ugly, the little black girl,
> really ugly,
> and very black, like all the sins.
> But you smile
> and it is a festival of angels.
> Sweetness of your white eyes,
> purity of your white teeth,
> I shall sing of you, little black girl, it is your turn now.
> I shall speak of the grace of your body, straight as a
> palm tree,
> but supple as a flame. (qtd. in Coulthard, *Race*, 91)

Here the black/white opposition does not merely create a "transparent" visual contrast. The poem's reaffirmation of the stereotypical associations of black and white undermines the potentially radical function of the celebration (implicit in the announcement "it is your turn now"). Ironically, therefore, it is in the black woman's white smile, white eyes, and white teeth that beauty resides. In the end, the speaker has reproduced the very discourse that he set out to subvert. He still acquiesces to the notion that beauty is white and therefore cannot be represented by black racial features.

H. G. DeLisser's *Pysche* (1959), a historical romance set in Jamaica during slavery, illustrates how such subconscious racial prejudice may subvert a potentially redemptive project. DeLisser's narrator describes the female slave protagonist as strikingly beautiful, but is at pains to establish that her beauty resides in her "non-Negroid" features:

> "There's a strain of Arab blood in her," the master had said more than once, glancing at her long hair, thin lips; "she isn't the pure McKay."
>
> "Perhaps, sir," had once ventured a junior officer, "she is the daughter of a chief."
>
> "That's what every one of them will say after they have been a year in Jamaica," laughed the captain; "everybody wants to be the son or daughter of a chief. But being that would not give this girl the features and hair she has. No. I guess there's Arab blood in her though her complexion is quite black. She has longish, soft hair; then look at her nose; it is positively hooked." (By this he meant that the girl's nose was more inclined to be aquiline than platerine or flat.) "She's good-looking too." (10)

The novelist is earnest in his praise of Psyche's beauty as an individual black woman, but equally emphatic in his denial of the beauty of black slave women in general: "Lithe, tall, with shining eyes, ebony in hue but with the telltale nose that spoke of her partly Semitic extraction, she was striking to look at in comparison with the other women on the estate" (19).

A less subtle deprecation of the *mulata*'s black heritage and the attribution of dichotomous moral values to black and white still appear as late as the 1940s in the literature of the Spanish Caribbean. In the poem "Yelidá" (1942), Tomás Hernández Franco of the Dominican Republic embodies two extreme racial and cultural stereotypes in Madam Suquí, the former Haitian prostitute, and Erick, the blond Norwegian sailor. He portrays both in terms that correlate their physical traits with their moral character. Erick is white, blond, and blue-eyed; his heart is pure:

> Erick, that young Norwegian lad
> with the soul like a fjord and a heart of mist.
> (qtd. in Morales, 207)

Madam Suquí is black and depraved:

> Madam Suquí once known as Mademoiselle Suquiete
> a virgin let loose on the village docks
> a creature of midnight at every hour. (qtd. in Morales, 209)

Their love affair is a symbolic struggle in which black evil vanquishes white innocence. The speaker also has recourse to the cultural stereotype that links Haitian blacks to the practice of witchcraft. While he evokes pity for the hapless Erick, more than a little Negrophobia colors his representation of the sorceress Madam Suquí.

"Yelidá" also exemplifies the xenophobia that compounds racial attitudes in the Dominican Republic, where blacks are considered less African and therefore superior to blacks from Haiti and other areas of the Caribbean. The racial prejudice implied in the poem is also evidence of the historical antipathy felt by Dominicans for Haitian blacks. Their hostility dates back to the Revolution of 1791, led by the Haitian slaves, and was born out of fear of the subversive effect of the revolt on slaves in other territories. The conflict was further exacerbated by the Haitian domination of Santo Domingo from 1795 to 1844.

Images such as the one offered by Hernández Franco are rare in the poetry of the twentieth century. More typical is the approach of the poet whose objective is racial redemption and the rejection of the Eurocentric model of female beauty. "Nubian Venus" (Venus nubia), a poem published in 1959 by the Puerto Rican José de Diego Padró, reflects a consciousness of the need to change the racial values implanted by slavery and colonialism:

> Sweet friend you will see how the good muses
> help me to shape these short couplets,
> Which in homage to Venus, matchless and divine,
> I engrave in lofty Alexandrine meter.
> But not to the white Venus do I sing my simple song;
> Not to the haughty Venus of Classical nudity,

Whose skin the milky swell of countless centuries
has anointed with spurious tongues;
Not to the great Nordic, Phoenician, or Roman Venus,
But to the Nubian Venus, Venus of brown skin,
Though brown, and though Nubian
Let her not envy the fairer Venus.
Give praise, then, to that goddess, the goddess of cinnamon,
The one who at one stroke all the senses bewitches.
Let loose a thousand pigeons for her.
Improvise chants and burn incense.
Give praise to that giant of boundless spirit,
From whose womb life flows like a river,
Whose breast is always fertile, whose form is stately,
For she is the source of your fighting race,
Your dark race, of sovereign and fecund impulse
Which one day will sustain the pillars of the world.
(qtd. in Morales, 78)

The speaker has deliberately avoided the practice of aesthetic subordination of the nonwhite woman. But because he is aware of doing the untoward, he still feels obliged to resort to the familiar to make the unfamiliar intelligible. He seeks to bestow poetic dignity on this woman by invoking the figure of the Greek goddess Venus. In a mildly satirical gesture the poet rejects this icon of female beauty that the high tradition of Western culture has consecrated. He replaces it with the brown-skinned Venus whom he proceeds to exalt.

On one level, this may be seen as an expression of the weariness with the values of Western civilization that produced the European Negro vogue in the early twentieth century. It may also be viewed as an attempt to counteract the sense of black inferiority that is contingent upon the ideology of white supremacy. More specifically, it signals a desire to replace an alienating and inaccessible white aesthetic ideal with a symbol of dark-skinned beauty that is more appropriate to Caribbean racial reality. By using pluralism rather than hierarchy as the basis of his comparison, the speaker contests the notion of the dark-skinned woman as an aberration from the Western norm. He images the "fair" Venus not as an absolute aesthetic ideal, but as a culturally defined icon. Equal aesthetic validity can therefore be claimed for the "dark" Venus: "Though brown, and though Nubian / Let her not envy the fairer Venus." Thus, the speaker achieves aesthetic differentiation without the discriminatory implications suggested by the last poem.

However, the method used to achieve a positive revaluation still reflects a lack of correlation between the poem's aesthetic discourse and its ideology. In the first place, by his use of "Alexandrine meter," the speaker shows his deference to one of the most hallowed European poetic conventions. Consequently, he betrays his lingering submission to the hegemonic tradition he seeks to subvert. To extol black beauty, he has appropriated the discourse traditionally used to pay homage to the emblem of white beauty. His tribute to the new icon retains both the mythic perceptions and the reverential posture assumed for the celebration of the original model.

To invest his black version with the high aesthetic value of the original, the speaker exploits the phonetic similarity between the Spanish words *nubia* and *rubia*. While the second adjective denotes color (blond), the first is an index of nationality (Northeastern African). But the poet relies, in part, on this phonetic association to confer on *nubia* the aesthetic prestige already possessed by the epithet *rubia*. Although the black woman is elevated to a mythic status and though the icon is Africanized by the epithet *nubia,* the speaker still perceives her from a position within the inherited European tradition. Such a strategy bears witness to one of the contradictions that have beset the decolonization process: the effort to establish a Caribbean identity has not always been attended by a radical break with alienating European modes of thought. Rather than creating new models, this effort has sometimes resulted in the mere transposition of foreign cultural models to local reality.

The colonial vestiges evident in "Venus nubia" coexist, nevertheless, with signs of ideological resistance. Although the poem is unambiguous in its celebration of the beauty of the black woman, the final section shows an unwillingness to reduce her to a passive aesthetic object to be contemplated and adored. Again, as in Lloréns Torres's "Black Woman" (La negra), the poet shifts from a purely aesthetic perspective to a view of the black woman as procreator and historical agent. By ascribing a creative function to the black Venus, Padró has modified significantly the original representation of Venus, with whom this function is not normally associated. This, in turn, is both a tacit assertion of the sterility of the culture that the icon represents and a reaffirmation of the stereotype that links the Negro to the creative life force. However, the poet attaches a special note to the creative role. The black Venus becomes the symbolic black mother of future liberators of black people—a political dimension that separates the image even further from its original model.

Like Padró, Barbadian poet H. A. Vaughan, writing in 1945, celebrates the beauty of the dark-skinned woman in the following early nationalist poem, to which he gave the telling title "Revelation":

Turn sideways now and let them see
What loveliness escapes the schools,
Then turn again, and smile, and be
The perfect answer to those fools
Who always prate of Greece and Rome,
"The face that launched a thousand ships,"
And such like things, but keep tight lips
For burnished beauty nearer home.
Turn in the sun, my love, my love!
What palm-like grace! What poise! I swear
I prize these dusky limbs above my life.
What laughing eyes! What gleaming hair! (1)

The ideological content and propagandistic motives of this poem are explicitly stated. Beginning with its title, it signals a will to counter the white supremacist colonial ideology by proclaiming the beauty of the woman of African descent. Yet the use of euphemistic neoclassical imagery ("dusky limbs" and "burnished beauty") suggests that the poet has at his disposal only a colonial discourse with which to challenge a colonial ideology.

Cuban poet Nicolás Guillén dedicated a poem in 1979 to the African American political activist Angela Davis, in which he achieves a more succinct form of aesthetic vindication:

I have not come here to tell you that you are beautiful.
I think that you are, that you are beautiful,
but that is not the reason. (qtd. in Morales, 369)

His de-emphasizing of the black woman's racial-aesthetic attributes derives, in part, from the Marxist-Leninist worldview that subsumes the race question under the notion of class conflict, which Guillén espoused at this point. But his simple formulation expresses eloquently his feeling of confidence regarding the black woman's beauty. Because he perceives it as given, it does not require defense or reinforcement.

In the preceding portraits the Afro-Caribbean woman appears as aesthetic object and voiceless Other. In 1938 Puerto Rican poet Julia de Burgos gave the woman of African descent a voice to define her racial identity. "Ay, ay, ay de la grifa negra" presents a vigorous assertion of racial pride by a black female persona. Like Guillén's poem to Angela Davis, this poem validates the beauty of the black woman without referring or submitting to the dominant white ideal:

> Ay, ay, ay, I am black, pure black;
> kinky hair and Kaffir lips;
> and flat Mozambican nose.
> A jet black woman, I cry and I laugh
> at the thrill of being a black statue,
> of being a piece of the night,
> where my white teeth flash like lightning;
> and being a black whip
> that is twisted on blackness
> to form the black nest
> where the crow lies.
> Black piece of blackness where I carve myself,
> ay, ay, ay, for my statue is all black
> . . . .
> Ay, ay, ay, the sins of the white king,
> let the black queen wash them in forgiveness
> . . . .
> Ay, ay, ay, my black race is slipping away
> running with the white race to become brown;
> to become the race of the future,
> fraternity of America! (qtd. in Morales, 157–58)

Two separate but related issues are foregrounded in this instance—one pertains to the black woman's racial identity, and the other to her participation in the national community. For the first thirteen lines the speaker concentrates on subverting the ideology of black racial inferiority. The poem is unique in its time for the revolutionary meaning it imparts to the established discourse. By using racially discriminatory epithets to designate her Negroid features, but simultaneously stripping them of their deprecatory connotations, the persona manages to articulate the discourse without authenticating it. Julia de Burgos employs a strategy distinctly different from that used in the poems of Muñoz del Monte and Sánchez-Galarraga. Their speakers defined the *mulata* as an aberration from the white norm. The black woman in this poem does not acknowledge the objective existence of such a norm. Instead she skillfully transforms the discourse of racial disparagement into affirmation of racial pride. Divesting the traditionally depreciated aspects of her physiognomy (thick lips, flat nose, kinky hair) of their negative aesthetic value, she reconstitutes them as signs of an African identity (Kaffir lips and Mozambican nose).

The speaker is also forthright in rejecting the euphemistic epithets used to avoid reference to blackness. Her designation of herself as "pure black" readily distinguishes her from the racially ambiguous *mulata*. She declares her blackness unequivocally and without apology, through the repetitive use of the word "negro" or other vocabulary denoting blackness in all but two of the poem's first thirteen lines. This assertive gesture is at once an act of defiance and an expression of triumph. A similar significance attends the declaration, "A jet-black woman, I cry and I laugh / at the thrill of being a black statue." By exalting her pure blackness, she rejects implicitly the inferiority complex that motivates efforts by many blacks to "whiten" the race. The persona has successfully resisted the pressure to conform to the white ideal. Her tears are not those of a black woman who feels victimized, but a statement of deeply felt racial pride. Her cry "Ay, ay, ay" is not a lament but a cry of celebration.

Through this persona, Julia de Burgos therefore offers an example of how the black woman, though historically subordinated because of her race, can repudiate the view of her blackness as the antithesis of the white aesthetic ideal. She has consciously assumed the role of maker of her own image: "Black piece of blackness where *I carve myself*" (emphasis mine). Beyond this, the poem also demonstrates that the "reality" of the black woman's racial and aesthetic inferiority has been socially constructed by those who have traditionally held power over her. It therefore opens the possibility of self-validation through the creation of an alternate Africa-centered ideology of blackness. A parallel to this stance is to be found in the response of black activists in North America in the 1960s. Like Marcus Garvey, their predecessor, they sought to undermine the intention and effect of white racist discourse by exhorting Negroes to assume their blackness with pride. De Burgos has turned the conventional representation of blackness on its head, erasing obliquely both the moral stigma attached to blackness and the representation of virtue as white. This she achieves by placing the black woman in a position where she can respond with magnanimous forgiveness to the crimes that her former white master perpetrated against her.

The final eight lines speak to the question of racial assimilation as it relates to the black woman. Julia de Burgos recognizes the reality of racial hybridity, but the introduction of this notion after the affirmation of black identity is significant. Her perspective of the Afro-Caribbean woman's racial identity echoes Raymond T. Smith's comment on the multiracial notion of the Caribbean. He maintains that "before ethnic identity can be transcended it must be asserted, . . . in order to ensure the stature, participation and self-respect of everyone in the local community" (54). The statement being made in De Burgos' poem, likewise, is that assimilation of the black woman must be preceded by appreciation of her blackness. Only then will it be an expression of true unity.

The recurrence of racial affirmation as a theme in these representations of the Afro-Caribbean woman has been a natural reactive response. Its aim has been to reclaim the power of self-definition that the white colonizer had appropriated. Essentially, the enterprise has been part of a process of self-differentiation, of establishing an image of the Caribbean person as distinct from the colonial master. An important observation to be made about the preceding depictions is that the beauty of the Afro-Caribbean woman is not always defined monolithically. Léon-François Hoffmann has noted a parallel practice among male Haitian poets. European French poetry, Hoffmann notes, defines feminine beauty as "formal harmony" and as having purely aesthetic value, like a work of art. For the Haitian poet, in contrast, movement is an essential component of beauty: "The poet does not seek to turn a woman into a painting, even less into a statue. What he wants to translate is, on the contrary, her vitality" (106). Poets of the Spanish-speaking Caribbean have given sexual overtones to this energy.

2

Sexual Myths and National Icons

Most distinctive and pervasive among the representations of the woman of African descent in Spanish Caribbean literature are those that center on her sexuality. These portrayals have perpetuated the long-standing myths men have created about woman as an essentially sexual creature. In this mythic view female sexuality signifies danger. H. R. Hays's extensive exploration of the myth of feminine evil reveals that across cultures and history male fantasy has given rise to a misogynist tradition based on such a perception. According to Hays, studies of Greek civilization have shown that "intense misogynist tendencies transformed the lure of the female body into an organ of danger and turned the sexual attraction of women into a malicious temptation" (85). Judeo-Christian ideology has further entrenched the myth by equating woman, sex, and sin, and by incorporating it into its ethical code. This male hostility, Hays notes, has been expressed either as fear or as sexual aggression. Both attitudes are apparent in Spanish Caribbean representations of women of African descent.

Although the eroticization of the female body has a long history in other older literary traditions, Western culture racialized the sexual myth. By the nineteenth century the generic definition was applied to the black female specifically. Sander Gilman, in his analysis of nineteenth-century European art, traces the notion of the black woman's body as an icon of sexual aberration back to the Middle Ages and early European travel literature (209). He notes that the black female body held great curiosity value for Victorian England. The correlation that society made between anatomical difference and difference in sexual behavior led to the reduction of the black female (symbolized by the Hottentot woman) to her sexual organs (212–13).

Vestiges of this general ethos survived in the *negrista* depictions of the rumba dancer in the 1920s and 1930s. But the antecedents of the image can be found in the nineteenth century, when writers established sensuality as a category for representing the *mulata*. Implied in this sexualized construction of race is the desexualization of white women that Romantic literary discourse had engendered. The fiery sensuality of the "dark woman" depended for its expression on the contrasting coldness of the "fair lady." In his 1873 novel *El negro Francisco,* Cuban writer Antonio Zambrana invokes the stereotype in his description of the mulatto slave, Camila: "There was a poisonous electricity in the demeanor of that woman. The sternest man could not look at her with impunity. How terrible is the torment of the man who spends his life abstaining rigorously from all but the purest emotions, when he stumbles on one of these beauties. They make us feel the fire of desire rather than heaven's divine fire burning in our veins!" (48). Camila struggles unsuccessfully to be located within the boundaries of Romantic purity. But her sensuality, as the novelist constructs it, is an inescapable condition and a curse.

Zambrana is at pains to exempt Camila from guilt for this biologically determined "sin." Her pure intentions notwithstanding, her flesh is her doom: "She would have wished to be an angel inspiring immaculate yearnings, and she was the devil inducing shameful fantasies. She would have wished to be the image of chastity, and she was the statue of temptation. This she was in spite of herself; she could not escape it" (48). What the speaker seeks to define as an inherent trait is the creation of a specific viewer. The novel itself establishes the status of the eroticized *mulata* as a white male fantasy since Francisco, the noble black slave who loves Camila, strips her of carnality and clothes her in Romantic garb: "Above all he loved her perfect purity, her virginal blushes and her chaste thoughts" (56).

Poets of the nineteenth century also reproduced this carnal image of the *mulata* and sustained it through their frequent recourse to metaphorical vocabulary underlining her deadly allure. This discourse manifests the ambivalent response of the white elite group to the racial transformation of Cuban society. The sexual danger projected onto the *mulata* reflects the fear of the social threat they perceived in the racial grouping to which she belonged. But the fight-or-flight response that such fear might have prompted was thwarted by their more powerful visceral sexual attraction to the *mulata* as an individual.

In Creto Gangá's 1847 poem "La mulata," the speaker studiously constructs an image of the *mulata* as a deviation from the traditional concept of womanhood: "more than woman she seems / the way she wiggles her hips" (qtd. in Morales, 310). In this tacit sexualization of the contrast between the "fair lady" and the "dark woman," there is even an undercurrent of allusions to the figure of the witch. The *mulata* does not fit into the mold of the desexualized white female, hence the hyperbole of the imagery and the association of her person with the violent aspects of nature:

> She is the one, in short, who thinks
> very little of the pavement
> where she walks,
> and the waggles of her hips
> wherever she goes
> shake shutters, awnings and signboards.
> A log lashed
> by wind and tide;
> . . . .
> Wild cane swayed
> by whirlwinds. (qtd. in Morales, 310–11)

So sensationalist a description of the hip-swaying *mulata*'s earth-shaking impact provides one example of the imaginative excesses to which their fascination with her sensuality led some nineteenth-century poets. In this account her sexual identity, like her racial identity, is not only dual but also unstable. She represents sexual potential, doubling as both erotic object and sexual agent, at once pleasurable and lethal. What the images of turbulence convey is not the *mulata*'s objectively sexual character but the speaker's own investment of eroticism in her, and the turbulent sexual feelings she arouses in him.

The subsequent ambivalent sexual characterization also reflects the speaker's love-hate response to the *mulata*. These images, like that of the honeysweet poison, foreground her potential for both pleasure and destruction:

> pepper that pleases the eye
> but sets the mouth on fire;
> liqueur with soothing smell
> and intoxicating effect;
> Spanish fly that sometimes vivifies
> and sometimes kills. (qtd. in Morales, 310)

Two attitudes are evident in this poetic fantasy: although the *mulata's* sensuality excites the speaker, he also betrays his sexual anxiety, his fear of his own desire. By placing sexual contact with the *mulata* off limits, the poet has transposed into his poem the social restrictions that the white ruling class in nineteenth-century Cuban society placed on the mulatto class, and their fear of the danger they sensed in this group. While recognizing the *mulata's* sexual appeal, the speaker also ascribes to it a capacity for destruction. He draws a metaphorical line between the permissible and safe (stimulation of sexual desire through fantasy), on the one hand, and, on the other, the forbidden (the unbearably intense but dangerous pleasure that he imagines can be derived from real sexual contact with the *mulata*). All the sexual metaphors are chosen appropriately to heighten this inflated image of her sexual power, from the relatively mild liqueur to the potently stimulating but potentially deadly aphrodisiac.

Inherent in this representation is a warning against sexual liaisons with the *mulata*. It is issued presumably to white men in nineteenth-century Cuba, since neither the literature nor the society of the time showed the mulatto woman as similarly affecting black or mulatto men. In fact, the norms of this racially divided society encouraged marriage within the boundaries of the individual's race. However, the felt need to issue such a warning is testimony to the *mulata's* incursion into the body of the white community through this sexual avenue.

A contemporary poem repeats this discourse, which suggests that the image had achieved some degree of standardization. Muñoz del Monte also characterizes the *mulata's* sexuality as "wine that sweetens and kills / if drunk to the last drop" (qtd. in Morales, 195). Unlike Crespo Borbón, however, he is reluctant to admit the possibility of any positive value in the *mulata's* sexuality. In "La mulata" (1845) he uses volcanic and fire imagery to promote the notion of her sexuality as a destructive force:

the sirocco wind blows fire in her skin,
laughter nestles on her lips
and lava bubbles in her breast.
Aphrodite's girdle encircles her;
not the girdle of myrtle and roses,
but a red-hot circle of fire
which consumes the unwary one who touches it.
. . . .
And in each turgid ball

of her trembling breast,
smooth, elastic, throbbing,
with a living magnetism
swells a fluid vortex. (qtd. in Morales, 196–97)

Muñoz's choice of imagery reflects, on the one hand, the continuing cultural dominance of the European worldview in the references to Venus and Aphrodite. But although Western culture provides his ultimate reference point, the speaker is aware of the need to modify its traditional images to distinguish the Caribbean subject. Thus, he transforms Aphrodite's girdle of myrtle and roses into a circle of burning fire, reinvesting the *mulata* with signs that heighten her destructive sexuality. As in the preceding poem, the real fear of the social danger represented by the increase of the mulatto class is entwined with this perception of sexual danger.

Through their portrayals of the rumba dancer, the *negrista* successors to these nineteenth-century poets crystallized the reductive image of the dark-skinned woman that the Western imagination had created. Hyperbole persists as a typical feature of the sexual discourse in *negrista* poetry. But the humor of the nineteenth-century caricature seems benign in comparison to the grotesquely exaggerated images painted by the *negrista* poets. Their trademarks are explicit references to the black woman's sexual parts:

How black Tomasa dances the rumba!
how José Incarnación dances the rumba!
She moves one rump, and then the other.
he stretches, crouches, thrusts out his haunches,
he thrusts out his belly, stoops, walks
on one heel, then on the other.
Chaqui, chaqui, chaqui, charaquí!
Chaqui, chaqui, chaqui, charaquí!
The powerful haunches of that girl Tomasa
turn with whirlpool fury
on an invisible axis,
matching in rhythm and with lewd dislocation
the lustful attack of Che Incarnación

. . . .

Black Tomasa with a lewd gesture,
moves her hip aside, raises her head,
and arms held high, hands joined,

resting on the nape of her ebony neck;
obscenely she thrusts out her round breasts.
(qtd. in Morales, 329–31)

This detailed verbal recreation of the Afro-Cuban dance is one of the earliest and most frequently cited poems that established the rumba dancer as a standard poetic figure. It illustrates the typical discursive strategy used by *negrista* poets to disseminate their perception of the black woman.

Published in 1928 by Cuban poet José Zacarías Tallet, this poem, entitled "Rumba," is impressive in its descriptive brilliance. It captures the drama and excitement of the event, reproducing very graphically the musical rhythms and providing a close-up view of the movements, minute gestures, and expressions of the dancers. Tallet dispenses with the metaphorical language of his nineteenth-century predecessors and creates the impression of the poet as a neutral transmitter of ethnographic information. Such a representation is so powerfully seductive that Rosa Valdés-Cruz characterizes it as a cinematographic replication of the dance (*Poesía*, 60).

However, claims of transparent realism obscure those features of the language that reflect the speaker's prejudice. Tallet's representation is striking, not so much because of the directness of the references to erotic body signs, but more because of the derogatory implications of the crude or animal terms he uses to designate them. Earlier poets had felt constrained to use more euphemistic expressions. They had created their image of the *mulata* as a sexual sensation obliquely, through metaphors and abstract analogies, and represented her sensuality without derogatory references to her sexual parts. Where those poets had alluded to her "hips" and "waist," the bolder poets of the twentieth-century movement were irresistibly drawn to the woman's buttocks, which they depicted using crude sexual references and words with bestial connotations, such as "rump" and "haunches."

Viewed from the perspective of its positive significance, this stereotype was a revolutionary celebration of eroticism, a glorification of the black woman's sexual physiognomy. Besides, the sexually explicit vocabulary reflected the general reaction against the bourgeois sense of decency during this period, and was specifically a defiant insertion of the carnality of the female body that had been expunged from Romantic literary discourse. The *negrista* movement was a propitious gesture to promote the woman of full African ancestry and to provide an antidote to the nineteenth-century preference for the *mulata*. It also gave expression to the desire to decolonize Caribbean culture and to highlight the African roots of national life.

This purpose, however, was largely undermined by the means used to achieve it. By their frequent recourse to animal vocabulary, *negrista* poets reflected their atavistic adherence to eighteenth-century European perceptions of the African woman's body. Europeans had not only compared her body negatively with that of the white woman, but had considered it akin to that of female animals. With their representations the *negrista* poets demonstrated that the sexually degrading stereotype survived the historical context in which it originated. Their deromanticization of the rumba dancer's body showed remarkable continuity with the voyeurism in Victorian England's response to Sarah Bartmann, the Hottentot woman who was displayed in that society as a spectacular example of anatomical abnormality and sexual deviance. Sander Gilman notes a special obsession in nineteenth-century Europe with the black woman's buttocks as a displacement for the genitalia (219). Caribbean *negrista* poets stand out because of the consistency with which they displayed this fascination. They used the rumba dancer to epitomize black female sexuality, and she became, in effect, their symbol of the black woman.

Further proof of the racist motive underlying this representation is the fact that white poets writing about white women did not resort to such degrading terminology. In essence, the image exacerbates the polarization of white and nonwhite that, as we saw, was the basis of the ethno-racial and aesthetic iconography. Implied in such depictions is a view of the black woman, with her uninhibited display of erotic energy, as the antithesis of the sexually restrained white woman. Thus, the *negrista* poets displaced onto the "dark woman" the taboo terms they could not apply to the "fair lady." But there is a more insidious racism embedded in this sexual discourse. Although the Cuban writers had incorporated the black woman into the literary mainstream, the discrimination that had originally excluded her persisted. They associated the grossly bestial imagery more with the black "wench" and less with the mulatto "favorite."

White Puerto Rican poets occupy a special place among the *negrista* perpetuators of the sexual myth. To a greater extent than others, Luis Palés Matos resorted to an Africanized discourse to create an exotically sexual black woman. The Queen of Tembandumba in the poem "Black Majesty" (Majestad negra, 1934) is one such figure:

Swinging her butt the Queen advances,
and from her huge haunches flow
sexy waggles thickened by the drumbeat
into rivers of sugar and molasses.
Black sugar mill of a sensual sugar harvest
her hips, churning and churning
ooze rhythms, bloody sweat
and the grinding ends in a dance.
Along the brightly-lit Antillean street
goes Tembandumba of Quimbamba
Flower of Tortola, rose of Uganda. (156)

The imagery of the last line quoted depicts the woman as magnificent and beautiful, and suggests an attitude of frank celebration and admiration in the viewer. But this impression is eroded by the poem's general objectification of the woman. This is the effect, for example, of the equation of her hip movements with a sugar mill churning out "rivers of sugar and molasses." The reference to her haunches further debases her to the level of a grotesquely sensual animal, and the use of the verb *culipandeando* in the original Spanish (from *culo*, a taboo word for the anus or buttocks) serves to vulgarize her sexuality. Because of the incongruity of this portrait with the connotations of exquisite refinement evoked by her royal title, it creates the effect of a deprecatory caricature even more grotesque than the caricature of early Spanish peninsular writers.

"Bombo" (1930), another poem by Palés Matos, effects a similar transformation of the black woman into an erotic body. This time she appears in the context of African savagery:

Come, brothers, to the celebration,
Dance the black god's dance
around the fire
where the white prisoner burns.
Let the most beautiful maiden
rip her flesh apart, open her sex
and let in the most virile warrior
to impregnate her. (Palés Matos, 154)

The Africanized dancer in "The Black Woman Sings to the White Ant" (La negra canta a la hormiga blanca, 1945), by Vicente Palés Matos, embodies a monstrously bestial sexuality:

Among the warriors Gonkula dances . . .
Black, Kaffir pearl, in her heat she exudes
a smell of fruit and mud, and she howls
like a jackal

. . . .

The warriors sing, and amid the hoarse beat of the drum
rises the lewd cry of a wild beast;
to the rhythm of the *son*
the black woman dances like a panther.
Her huge hips, her fruity bosom
and her sex like a fierce cactus. (qtd. in Morales, 106)

As in "Black Majesty," there is a dissonance in the imagery associated with the black dancer in this poem. The predominance of stereotypical images of African savagery eclipses any favorable connotations borne by the "Kaffir pearl" image. In addition, the bizarre metaphorical reference to her genitals as a "fierce cactus" betrays both the irresistible curiosity of the sexual voyeur, and his fear of what he imagines is the monstrous and dangerous sexuality of the "savage" woman.

Though they sometimes dispensed with this Africanist discourse, other poets of the period who wrote about local dancers still perpetuated the sexual myth. In "The Black Woman Dances the *Son*" (Baila la negra el son), one of the earliest *negrista* poems in which the figure of the black dancer appears, Francisco Negroni Mattei emphasizes the hypnotic effect of her erotic body signs:

The black woman dances the *son*
with her naked belly
and her round buttocks. (qtd. in Morales, 48)

Although the more flagrantly bestial imagery has been normally associated with the black woman, Angel de Angel is daring and contemptuous in his sexual caricature of the *mulata* dancing the *bomba*:

This wild
black-assed
hot mulatta

. . . .

This round-rumped gal
dances the *bomba*. (qtd. in Morales, 155)

And Dominican poet Manuel del Cabral is aroused by the "stormy motions" of the mulatto dancer's "haunches" (qtd. in Morales, 221.)

Images such as these suggest that the Afro-Caribbean woman excited both the fancy and the desire of her creators. In her they perceived and experienced, vicariously, uninhibited sexual pleasure. But they did not consider the "genteel" discourse that euphemizes human eroticism an appropriate vehicle for their representations. Any potential for celebrating the release from sexual inhibition that she symbolized was therefore largely vitiated by this unrestrained, and at times crude, language. The poets succeeded in authenticating rather than in transforming a discourse that has been used historically to degrade the sexuality of the woman of African descent.

Nowhere is this better illustrated than in the unsavory connotations borne by the pervasive sensory imagery in *negrista* verse. For example, the references to squalor and bestiality in José Tallet's "Rumba" betray aloofness and even repulsion in the speaker:

and there is a smell of jungle
and there is a smell of sweat
and there is a smell of men
and there is a smell of women
and there is a smell of city tenements. (qtd. in Morales, 331)

Similar references to dirt, offensive smells, and unpleasant body odors recur in other poems. Vicente Palés Matos, for example, evokes the "Kaffir pearl" who smells of fruit and mud, and in Luis Palés Matos's "Black Town" (Pueblo negro, 1926) the black woman smells "of earth, of wild beast, of sex" (qtd. in González and Mansour, 154). In "Black Majesty" (Majestad negra) the bloody sweat of the protagonist combined with the sugar and molasses oozing from her hips creates a distasteful mixture.

In addition, the repeated use of "lascivious" and "lewd" as adjectives to describe her and her movements is a symptom of the popularity of this uninviting image of the black woman's sensuality. These adjectives do not function as neutral erotic signifiers but have the connotations of wanton lust and sexual offensiveness with which Christian mythology has imbued them. In this we find further demonstration of the ability of myths and stereotypes to outlast historical change. The origins of the myth of black (and especially black female) sexual immorality go back to impressions formed and propagated by early European travelers in their first contact with the African's nakedness. Words such as "lewd," "wanton," and "lascivious" were standard in the vocabulary used to describe African women. The application of such terms to the Afro-Caribbean woman does not suggest that the *negrista* poets were subverting this earlier discourse.

A poem written by the Dominican poet Antonio Frías Gálvez, after the waning of the *negrista* movement, continues to perpetuate the stereotype of the black woman as a mindlessly sensual creature, totally given over to the frenzy of the dance and oblivious to all else:

> The Negress is dancing . . . !
> Ah Negress Chimbá!
> Ah Negress Chimbá!
> How cruel you are to that Negro
> who's watching you from afar!
> He offered to marry
> the Negress Chimbá;
> but she wants no children,
> she just wants to dance. (qtd. in Morales, 276–77)

Here the black dancer epitomizes freedom from repression and the release of the body from the dictates of labor. But by explicitly divorcing her sexuality from any reproductive function, it also reaffirms the myth of the sexualized woman as the opposite of the maternal woman.

Such images are largely, but not exclusively, the creation of the male imagination. They appear occasionally in the work of female poets. Carmen Cordero of Cuba, who was born in 1940, after the official end of the *negrista* movement, provides a contemporary example of a female poet who perpetuates that masculinist practice:

> Lewdly she writhes to the rumba beat
> like a tongue of red fire,
> and she wags her fat hips
> like a hammock tossed by a zephyr wind.
> The vigor of the rhythm
> floods her cinnamon body with diamonds,
> and she abounds in smells of the jungle
> from her head to her grimy slipper. (qtd. in Morales, 428)

The poet in this instance does not show the same fascination with the sexual signifiers of the female body, but the discourse being reproduced is that of the male *negrista* poets. For example, she has retained the earlier characterization of the dancer's sexuality as lust, and there is a hint of disgust in the allusions to dirt and the smells of the jungle. The use of this mode of representation by a female poet points to the fact that a monolithic gender analysis does not fully explain these eroticized images. Racial identity and class position have also compromised the transgressive potential of the discourse on the sexuality of the woman of African descent.

The preceding poems are examples of the voyeuristic postures assumed by some poets in their attempt to capture the Afro-Caribbean cultural ethos. In the process they show little sensitivity to, or understanding of, the scenes and people they describe. Yet these images find their roots in reality. In the Spanish Caribbean the majority of popular dancers have been black or mulatto. But white *negrista* poets propagated this image at the expense of others, and the manner of depiction frequently amounted to a denial of the woman's humanity. From their perspective the dancer was no more than a spectacle and, frequently, a form of comic entertainment. This *negrista* image reintroduced and added, albeit unintentionally, a vulgar dimension to the burlesque discourse of the earlier European Spanish tradition.

One function of stereotypes, even ostensibly favorable ones, is to ensure a certain role performance. This applies to the stereotype of the dancer that white *negrista* poets appropriated as a cultural symbol. Their insistent focus on this image and their exclusion of others reflect the desire of the dominant white group to carve out a restricted field for the self-actualization of the Afro-Caribbean woman. An insidiously conservative political agenda underlies the deceptively innocent façade of this image of the sexually alluring, happy rumba dancer. Poets chose this image because it was socially and politically nonthreatening. Glorification of the sexual stereotype was the kind of literary response that would not encourage any challenge to the social order. On the contrary, it seems designed to divert attention away from the dancer's social disadvantage by creating a picture of social integration.

Critical assessments of this sexual image in *negrista* poetry vary, depending on whether the critic chooses to legitimize the image or to deconstruct it. Some commentators have sought to obscure the poets' underlying derogatory attitudes by invoking the realist imperative. José Arrom's approving judgment of the image provides a remarkable example of the convergence of poetic and critical discourses: "But where there is the greatest difference in racial preferences is as regards the female figure. Slenderness, a swan's neck, palm-tree figure for the white man; powerful haunches, agile shoulders and, above all, buttocks: a big, fleshy, contractile black rump, for the black man" ("Poesía," 399). Discrimination inheres not in the content of this claim, but in the language in which the critic has formulated it. His intention is to apply the principle of cultural relativism to the different perceptions of the bodies of white and black women. Nonetheless, his appropriation of the very discourse that has been used to debase black female sexuality betrays his complicity with the caricature of the poets.

In 1935 Cuban anthropologist Fernando Ortiz added his voice to the chorus of the poets, though he couched his comments in ostensibly more objective critical rhetoric:

> This aesthetic concept of the big-rumped black woman and the sensual attraction of the butt-swinging *mulata* are . . . the product of the realist description of their anatomy and the powerful eroticism of the swaying carnality of their fleshy rumps. They are merely the genuine expression . . . of an uninterrupted tradition of representation of the black woman . . . which takes us back historically, ethnographically and artistically to the *Callipygian Venus,* to the frescoes on the tombs of the *mulatas* who were Egyptian queens. . . . When Antillean poets give realist verbal expression to their perceptions of the woman of African descent, they have had to use the same plastic elements artists used thousands of years ago to depict the Negroid woman and her pompous protuberances. ("Ultimos," 163)

Ortiz's comment attests to the seductive power of the stereotype and the readiness with which the myth has been accepted. Besides the effect of caricature that his explanation creates, Ortiz overlooks the fact that the sexualized black female body is a Western cultural construct, and that many *negrista* poets constituted black female sexuality as a sign of bestiality.

Ann Venture Young, in "Black Women in Hispanic American Poetry," comes closer to reflecting the complexity of the poets' attitude to the *rumbera*. She recognizes both the virtuosity of their descriptions and the dehumanizing function of the imagery. However, her conclusion that such representations reflect "exaltation of and an admiration for her as symbolic of what they [the poets] perceive as a life characterized by complete personal and sexual freedom" does not give adequate weight to the counterproductiveness of the discourse (25). While the poets are evidently projecting their own (suppressed) desires in their sexualization of the black woman, one needs to distinguish between the admiration of the detached voyeur, contemplating what to him is a marvelous monstrosity, on the one hand, and, on the other, admiration in the sense of feelings of approval. It is the former ambiguous sense of fascination and repulsion that typifies the attitude of some Euro-Caribbean *negrista* poets. One might reasonably conclude that they considered the sensuality of the black woman's body remarkable in the same terms that it was for nineteenth-century white Europeans.

Other critics, such as G. R. Coulthard, Lemuel Johnson, and Richard Jackson react less favorably to such portrayals. In *Race and Colour in Caribbean Literature,* Coulthard observes that in *negrista* iconography the rumba dancer appears distorted, disfigured, and grotesque, surrounded by an atmosphere of animal sensuality and violence. He recognizes a similar interest in the black woman's sensuality among French and English Caribbean poets, but he also finds that they do not reduce her to the level of a sexual animal without thought or feeling. His recognition of the presence of this perspective even in the work of the Afro-Cuban Nicolás Guillén counters the oversimplification of commentaries that categorize the images along the exclusive lines of the writer's racial background (94).

Richard Jackson and Lemuel Johnson have also cited the portrayal of the sensual rumba dancer to validate their strong criticism of the *negrista* movement for its caricatured, external, and one-dimensional view of the Negro. Richard Jackson notes that "they [white *negrista* poets] were given to promoting a one-dimensional image of the black as an unintellectual, sexual animal. The colored woman especially became a distorted figure not too far removed from the jungle" (*Black Image,* 43). Lemuel Johnson comments on the lack of moral concern accompanying the obsession with the erotic energy presumed to emanate from the black woman (*Devil,* 76). In a withering commentary on the expression of the Afro-Caribbean theme in the poetry of Luis Palés Matos, Johnson characterizes his "sexual slumming" as a vulgar approach to the 1920s Negro craze, and attributes the exotic-voyeuristic image to the dilettante explorer's search for the temporarily titillating ("*El Tema Negro,*" 123–36).

Part of the significance of the *rumbera* image lies in the indirect contrast it provides for the conventional image of female decorum and modesty. Cuban poet Rafael Esténger invokes this antithesis implicitly in "Dialogue" (Coloquio), published in 1934:

"Don't be vulgar, my dear Estrella
don't dance the rumba no more.

You're a lady and all now;
Now you are a School Teacher,
White folk will laugh
just seeing you dance." (qtd. in Morales, 344)

Esténger's poem reacts against the caricatured and sexually degraded stereotype of the *rumbera*. It also demonstrates the speaker's intuition of the potential use of the stereotype by whites to reinforce the notion of black inferiority. The black woman who has advanced socially through education must therefore relinquish the *rumbera* role that is associated with vulgarity and lower status.

But the discourse on sexuality is more complex in other poems, where signs of involvement with the *rumbera* temper the detached voyeurism of the male speaker. "Elegy for María Belén Chacón" (Elegía de María Belén Chacón, 1930) by the white Cuban poet Emilio Ballagas is evidence of this:

María Belén, María Belén, María Belén,
Marí Belén Chacón, María Belén Chacón, María Belén Chacón
with your butt swinging from side to side
from Camagüey to Santiago, from Santiago to Camagüey
. . . .
No longer will I see my instincts
in the happy round mirrors of your two buttocks.
Your constellation of curves
will light no more the sky of the dance. (qtd. in Morales, 384–85)

A major difference between this poem and those discussed previously is the explicit involvement of the speaker with the dancer. In this instance the mirror-reflection image indicates that the dancer provides vicarious sexual pleasure for the speaker and imaginary release of his sexual inhibitions. But this greater rapprochement is also accompanied by the caricature of her body movements ("with your butt swinging from side to side / from Camagüey to Santiago, from Santiago to Camagüey"). Here one senses the speaker's distance from the object of his gaze.

The myth of black female sexuality is not an exclusive creation of white male fantasy during the *negrista* years. As seen previously, at least one white female poet has helped to perpetuate the myth. Male Afro-Caribbean poets also show their fascination with the black dancer's sexual appeal and have even reproduced the bestial vocabulary. Nevertheless, there are certain nuances in some representations of this figure by the latter poets, which may be associated with the (racial) position from which they write.

In "Caridá" (1933), Cuban mulatto poet Marcelino Arozarena evokes the figure of the *rumbera* through the voice of a male speaker who bemoans her absence:

> Why does the daughter of Yeyemá not come to the celebration?
> the fleshy,
> the tasty,
> the happy and light-hearted Caridá?
> The mulatto girl that wears down her happy slipper
> with sensual rubbing
> and heavy stomping
> her rump nibbling and trembling,
> temptation to love.
> The awesome fit that shakes her being
> the electrifying swoon that sweetens her heart,
> bends her waist
> and squeezes her madly
> in the Ethiopian sweetness of the delicious *guaguancó*
> with the magic in the ebb of her sugary blood
> and the shivers of the lulling of the vibrating bongo drums.
> Why does rumba-dancing Caridá not come to the celebration?
> with her happy, teasing mulatto laugh
> "Guasa, Columbia, a conconcó mabó."
> when the rumba reaches frenzied heights,
> Why does the daughter of Yeyemá not come to the feast,
> the fleshy,
> the tasty,
> the happy, mischievous Caridá in dancing shoes?
> (qtd. in Morales, 402–3)

At first sight, the vocabulary of this description merely reproduces the voyeur's sensationalized stereotype. But there are indices of this spectator-speaker's involvement with the dancer, which the preceding poets do not express. For example, by adding the line "temptation to love," Arozarena modulates the bestial implications of the allusion to "her rump nibbling and trembling," which would otherwise make him indistinguishable from the white *negrista* poets. It suggests that the speaker views the dancer not merely as a sexual sensation but also as an individual with whom he can engage intimately. His attraction to her as a potential lover reduces the distance between the viewer and the viewed, which was evident in Ballagas's mirror-reflection image.

Arozarena displays his sensitivity to the African origins of the dance by depicting Caridá as the daughter of Yeyemá, the Yoruba goddess of rivers and springs. Thus, he offers an alternative to the exotic veneer in the African-sounding vocabulary of the poetry of Luis Palés Matos. Sylvia Wynter has noted the frequent misreading and distortion of the image of the dancer by *negrista* poets: "The stereotype of the dancing/singing minstrel 'over-saw' an important truth: the black transplanted the dance because it was a central part of the oral/ritual structure of his religious world. As time passed, and his origin became remote, the world of this symbolic universe deserted him.... Fragments, powerful ones, remained. The eye of the writer saw these fragments and used them either for art, ... or as the caricatured stereotype of ideology and the stock characters of inferior literature" (18–19). "Caridá" is a rare attempt to link the Cuban *rumbera* to this African religious world.

Of particular significance as it relates to the *negrista* revolt against bourgeois decorum is the association of the dancer in this poem with fruits, through the epithets "tasty," "fleshy," and "sweet." G. R. Coulthard notes that in European poetry woman's beauty is denoted by flowers, such as the lily, rose, and carnation. Most importantly, he adds that in Caribbean poetry "there is a significant change of emphasis in the attitude to the woman, for while flowers are appreciated for their beauty of shape and colour and in some cases their perfume, fruits and vegetables ... are eaten. So that the use of fruit analogies would seem to reflect a different attitude—an attitude of frank sensuality which ... is perhaps the predominant note in the West Indian attitude to life" (*Race,* 89–90).

But critics have diverged in their reactions to this use of fruit imagery. For Mónica Mansour it reflects a correlation of aesthetic discourse and nationalist ideology (172–81). Ann Venture Young, on the other hand, voices the classic feminist disapproval of the objectification implicit in the imagery that portrays the woman as "one more natural resource, sought after, cultivated, and exploited for the pleasure and satisfaction of the master" ("Black Woman in Afro-Caribbean Poetry," 140). However, the significant difference in Arozarena's use of fruit imagery is that it does not convey the sense of repulsion or crudity seen in the work of the white *negrista* poets, nor is the sexual degradation of the woman its effect. What emerges instead is the male persona's awareness of the dancer as a valued agent of sexual pleasure.

   Léon-François Hoffmann also notes the recurrence of the image of the
erotic black woman in Haitian poetry, but is careful to point out that the
effect is not to shock or demean. He identifies an even more extensive use
of fruit vocabulary by Afro-Haitian poets for whom the Haitian woman's
body becomes "a veritable basket of tropical fruits," and who equate the act
of love with the act of eating (102–5). The following poem is a parodic
illustration of this practice:

> When I see you I see the fruit of my country
> So juicy, so subtle and deliciously sweet;
> Your teeth make me think of young corns' pearly grains
> And on your breath wafts the perfume of our guavas.
> I have never touched your lips, your smooth arms,
> But when I see them so round, pure and firm of flesh
> I hunger to taste them as a traveller bites
> The mahogany apples that edge our country lanes
> . . . .
> Your bosoms are sisters of the marmalade plums
> Those fruits blond and heavy of our blessed land;
> . . . .
> But all these delicious fruits: meaty soursops,
> Coco plums and cinnamon apples and mangoes,
> All these fruits, I think, I really think
> Would I find if only I could taste your tongue.
> (qtd. in Hoffmann, 103–4)

   Nicolás Guillén, who offered alternatives to the prevailing aesthetic
images of the black woman, was also inspired to write about the *rumbera*.
In his "Rumba" (1931) the spectator-speaker shows even greater engagement with the dancer than the speaker of "Caridá":

> Pepper in your hips,
> flexible golden haunches:
> sweet rumba girl,
> naughty rumba girl.
> In the water of your robe
> float all my desires,
> sweet rumba girl
> naughty rumba girl.
> Desire to sink
> in that deep warm sea:

bottom
of the sea!

. . . .

I will have you tamed,
I will have you well tied,
when you come to my tenderness
as you run from it now. (I:123–24)

On one level, this view objectifies the dancer in terms similar to those
noted in some poems discussed previously. But again, as with Arozarena's
poem, the bestial implications of the reference to the dancer's haunches are
moderated by the description of them as flexible and golden. Through the
image of man taming a horse even though it is larger than himself, this
speaker appropriates the discourse of sex and power to express his response to the desire that the *mulata* stirs in him. Guillén's poem may even
appear to be a classic expression of misogyny.

Closer observation, however, reveals that for the speaker the *rumbera*
signifies more than a sexual spectacle or a sexual object to be dominated.
Forming a striking contrast to the mirror-reflection image in Ballagas's
poem is Guillén's use of water imagery. The mirror, symbolizing narcissistic sexual desire, reinforces the distance between the viewer and the dancer
and denies the possibility of a more than illusory contact through fantasy.
In contrast, the desire for sexual participation, conveyed in the image of
the deep, warm ocean in which the speaker in Guillén's poem yearns to be
immersed, and the gentleness of the allusion to sexual intimacy, are expressions generated in the consciousness of one who moves within the
rumbera's world.

Anglophone Caribbean poetry also offers an alternative to the re-
ductively sensual *negrista* image. Writing in 1922 about a black cabaret
singer-dancer, Claude McKay, a Jamaican poet living in the United States,
thematizes the difference between a voyeurism that focuses on the sensual
façade and the deeper concern of a speaker who intuits the sadness of the
real individual beneath the theatrical surface:

Applauding youths laughed with the young prostitute
And watched her perfect, half-clad body sway,
Her voice was like the sound of blended flutes
Blown by black players on a picnic day,
She sang and danced on gracefully and calm,
The light gauze hanging loose about her form;

To me she seemed a proudly swaying palm,
Grown lovelier from passing through the storm.
Upon her swarthy neck the black curls
Luxuriant fell; and tossing coins in praise
The wine-flushed, bold-eyed boys, and even the girls
Devoured her shape with eager, passionate gaze;
But looking at her smiling face,
I knew that she was not in that strange place. (42)

In other cases it is the religious or ritualistic meaning of the dance rather than the sensuality of the dancer's body that captures the poets' imagination. The Barbadian William Arthur's "Negro Lass" exemplifies this spirit:

Negro Lass with the skin of pearl,
Black as jade, and a jade this girl,
Blow the conchee, beat the drum,
Beat my heart, beat to your doom,
Beat the drums, beat!
Boom-boom! boom-boom!
Heart of a savage, eyes of a star,
Lithe as a panther. Africa! . . .
Negro lass! Negro lass! . . .
Roll your eyes; roll your hips,
Roll till the words beat past your hips,
There is a rhythm in my heart
Roll, roll, never to part—. . .
Roll, roll, Negro Boy! (qtd. in Figueroa, 12–13)

The speaker in Jamaican Philip Sherlock's "Pocomania" (1959), though positioned as a voyeur, understands the religious significance of the pocomania dancer's experience of spirit possession:

Black of night and white of gown
White of altar, black of trees
"Swing de circle wide again
Fall and cry me sister now
Let de spirit come again
Fling away de flesh an' bone
Let de spirit have a home." (qtd. in King, 60)

This poem bears out an observation made by Hoffmann about the representation of the voodoo dancer by some Haitian poets: "Despite her violent, often suggestive movements, the desirability of a dancing woman's body is no longer relevant; it becomes the medium that will allow the Gods to manifest their presence" (107).

A rare instance of the sexual representation of the Afro-Caribbean woman from the perspective of a female Afro-Caribbean poet is Puerto Rican Carmen Colón Pellot's "The Land Is a Mulatto Woman" (La tierra es una mulata, 1938):

> The land is a mulatto woman,
> a mulatto woman is the land
> with her strong, lustful smell
> and her cinnamon color.
> The hills are her warm breasts,
> breasts of a restless woman;
> breasts filled with green desire
> caressed and kissed by the sun.
> The fiery lashes
> leave her subdued and still;
> then the ploughing man
> sates his zestful appetite.
> The land is a mulatto woman,
> a mulatto woman is the land;
> with her springs of water-life,
> and her furrows in waiting. (49–50)

While this poet reproduces the *negrista* view of the *mulata*'s sexuality as wanton lust, she is mainly appropriating that long-standing Western patriarchal discourse that has identified woman with the land (nature) in its creative and nurturing functions. Colón Pellot confirms the stereotype of female sexual passivity and its antithesis, male sexual dominance. She has sought, however, to adapt the inherited convention to suit the local reality by her specific racial identification of the woman as mulatto. This representation affirms the creative possibilities of the *mulata*'s sexuality, thereby refuting the *negrista* vision of nonreproductive eroticism.

Because of the centrality of race in the discourse that has constituted the Negro, there are similarities in the depictions of both black men and black women. Sexualized male images, however, are rare in the work of female poets. In "Brown Adonis" (Pardo Adonis, 1937) Clara Lair of Puerto Rico creates a stereotypical image of the black male buck by resorting to a euphemistic discourse:

Swell, all alone, the dry river of my instinct
Swell my river and let it run loose to the lost forest
of the unknown!
The day, brown Adonis, where my stagnant weariness
is all white . . .
Weary of whiteness, of the colorless color . . . !
(qtd. in Morales, 46)

It is clear from these examples that this discourse on sexuality is predicated upon race rather than gender. However, it is the woman of African descent in particular who has come to embody nonwhite sexuality in Spanish Caribbean writing. When Lloréns Torres chooses a black man as subject, he defines him in terms of his physical and spiritual strength:

As a child, into the forest in the night I journeyed,
with the old Negro from the estate,
and together we crossed the thick swamp.
I heard the silent footsteps of the wild animals
and the warm breath of their open mouths.
But the Negro at my side was a tower of strength
who with his arms tore the cotton trees
and with his eyes swallowed up the dark.
As a man, again into the forest of the world did I go
. . . .
And I was afraid, as I was back then, . . . but I did not run away
for in my own shadow I always saw
the old Negro always at my side. (qtd. in Morales, 41–42)

Similarly, Evaristo Chevremont describes the black man's body in terms of its elemental strength:

The bodies of the Negroes, of virile texture,
appear naked among the thick plants,
fresh color, virgin flesh, perfect form.
Their bodies like hammers, their chests like shields.
(qtd. in Morales, 49)

In her study of slave women in the British Caribbean, Barbara Bush notes that the sexual myth, first propagated by European travelers of the fourteenth and fifteenth centuries, and fully entrenched in the colonial white mind by the end of the eighteenth century, was the most damaging to black women (*Slave,* 13). What the poems cited in this chapter have shown is the incredible longevity of this myth. Two types of erotic investment mark the relationship between the writers and their subjects: one mediated by voyeurism and the other by sexual desire. The white poets, their good intentions aside, have displayed their alienation from, and lack of understanding of, the Afro-Caribbean woman's cultural world. Their frequent posture of detachment, their expressions of aversion and ridicule, or, at best, the ambivalence of their love-hate responses separate them from those poets of African descent who, even while they reproduce certain features of the dominant discourse on the Afro-Caribbean woman's sexuality, seem to write from a position within her world.

Disgust and Desire: The Politics of Interracial Sex

White writers who perceive sensuality as the essence of the Afro-Caribbean woman have presented her in two postures: as sexual predator or as the object of sexual domination. Their projections of fear or unconscious desire frequently color (and cloud) their perceptions.

The poetry of the Dominican Republic provides two of the most elaborate representations of the Afro-Caribbean woman as a voracious and sadistic sexual animal who first seduces and then destroys her innocent, naive, white male victim. Francisco Muñoz del Monte's "La mulata" (1845) is unsurpassed in its hyperbolic depiction of the *mulata*'s sexuality. He orchestrates images of fires and volcanoes, as well as allusions to icons of feminine evil, to predispose the reader to accept the portrayal of the *mulata* as the dangerous seductress who leads to the white man's demise. While Crespo Borbón was content to give an abstract description of the *mulata*'s sexual character and its impact, Muñoz del Monte presents a highly dramatized and detailed account of the encounter between the *mulata* and her victim. She is cast in the role of the serpent preying on a defenseless bird:

> into the fatal mouth of the serpent
> the mighty bird fell.
> Then you will see him. In soft coils
> her arms entrap and crush him,
> they tie him, and entwine him, and compress him,
> they imprison him, and press him without mercy.
> . . . .
>
> And her trembling lips turn purple

and her rosy tongue turns black,
and flecks of foam appear
like white snow when the sun peeps through.

Elastic snake, hungry boa,
the *mulata* seizes her victim,
she crushes, squeezes, presses, entraps him,
in her frenzy she sucks, she licks, she bites

. . . .

And the frenzy grows and grows,
the moans grow louder, the struggle heightens,
the victim bites, shudders,
agonizes and will surely die.

Mercy, for God's sake, Mercy. Man is not made of stone,
pleasure has its limits,
shame and confusion on the wretched one
who crosses the barriers of pleasure.

Tempt him no more, Oh insatiable Circe

. . . .

No more, for God's sake, no more! Man is not made of stone.
There is only one made of bronze: the *mulata*
Useless plea. She feasts, then kills,
she opens and closes the tomb at will. (qtd. in Morales, 198–200)

Clear echoes of the myth of the dangers of female sexuality are discernible
in this account. It reproduces this image from eleventh- or twelfth-cen-
tury Europe: "A woman seeks her prey like the lion, scorches it to a cinder
with the fires of love, and finally bestows death and destruction like the
poison of the dragon" (Hays, 110–11). Muñoz del Monte's use of the
serpent analogy is not fortuitous. A phallic symbol, used in both Christian
and earlier mythologies, it serves to identify the *mulata* as the castrating
or sexually destructive woman.

All the signs of barbarism previously represented as the index of her
African heritage are invested in the *mulata's* sexual behavior. Another
effect of the poem is its confirmation of the stereotype of the *mulata* as
hypersensual, and its echoing of nineteenth-century beliefs about the dark
woman's insatiable sexual appetite. This attribute is also construed as an
enormity, as an aberration from acceptable human norms. But perhaps
what impresses the reader most are the exaggerated limits to which the

speaker finds it necessary to extend his imagination to fit the *mulata's* sexuality into his ideological system. Implicit in his posture is the puritanical belief that sexual pleasure has strict boundaries. The *mulata* is a source of excessive sexual ecstasy, and the man who falls for her charms violates the laws of Christian morality. In such a reenactment of the myth of the fall, the *mulata* becomes the new Eve. By portraying her as the white man's rapist, the poet has attempted to absolve the white man of the historical charge of violating black and mulatto women. This presentation of the *mulata* as the perpetrator of sexual violence on the white man also suppresses the paradoxical secret enjoyment on the part of the alleged victim. His agony is not the agony of pain; it is the agony of exquisite sexual pleasure.

Given the historical context of the poem, it is not difficult to understand the apparent sanction against aggressive female sexuality. Here, however, the attitude of the speaker is underlain by the commonly held nineteenth-century view that racial mixing was morally wrong. White Cuban society of the period condemned *mulatez* and expressed fears about the transformation of Cuba into "a sinful land of mulattoes." Thus, on the one hand, the *mulata* inherited the sexual stigma originating from the illegitimacy of the sexual union out of which she was born. On the other, the cataclysmic potential attributed to her sexual dominance in this poem is not only a product of the white man's sexual anxiety. It is also a masked expression of the real fear of social dominance that the white ruling class perceived in the disturbing numerical increase of mulattoes in colonial Cuba. As frequent consorts of white men, mulatto women were not surprisingly at the center of this social anxiety.

Through their representation of the *mulata's* sexual malignancy, writers participated subtly in the social construction of reality. Racist ideology in the nineteenth century led to public postures such as this claim that "the white race of men has drawn back in disgust from anything like general intermingling with the females of inferior races" (qtd. in Johnson, *Devil*, 59). A problem had arisen because of the discrepancy between such public posturing and the high incidence of sexual intermingling between white men and black or mulatto women. It is this contradiction between ideology and reality that has found its way into the literature. Not only the racist order of colonial society, but also its ideological underpinnings had to be perceived to remain intact. To admit to the reality of interracial sexual liaisons would threaten the whole racist theory with collapse. To circumvent this contradiction, the poet has created a counter-theory of reality. He has re-presented the white man, who was the historical epitome of social dominance and the frequent perpetrator of sexual violence on the mulatto woman, in the role of the sexually victimized, while depicting her sexuality as dangerous.

The reappearance of this sexual myth in the saga-like poem "Yelidá," published a whole century later by Tomás Hernández Franco, another poet of the Dominican Republic, illustrates its durability. "Yelidá" conjures up an image of the black woman as an evil witch who subjugates the white man with her supernatural sexual power. The poet weaves a mythic aura around this tale of the young Norwegian sailor who comes to Haiti, where the black ex-prostitute Madam Suquí bewitches and then seduces him. The poem underscores the "abnormal" circumstances under which he falls in love with her. He tries to exorcize his passion for her, but resistance is futile, and the evil power of her witchcraft overwhelms his white innocence and purity:

Erick loved Suquiete amid attacks of fever
shivers and faintings and drank quinine in great gulps of rum
to cast that black girl out of his flesh
to drive her out of his fair hair
so he could think of his Norwegian beach. (qtd. in Morales, 209)

As in the last poem, the myth of the Afro-Caribbean woman's sexual virulence creates the fiction of white male innocence. Incredible sexual naïveté is imputed to the Norwegian sailor: "he was twenty, a virgin in his plastic boots / and thought babies like fish were born" (qtd. in Morales, 208). The association between the two is reminiscent of Brabantio's theory of the Othello-Desdemona relationship in Shakespeare's *Othello*. Since, as Brabantio reasons, no "fair maid" could be naturally attracted to the "sooty bosom" of a Moor, such a union must have resulted from his use of supernatural methods of seduction. By casting the mulatto woman as a female version of Othello, Hernández Franco has obscured or, more perniciously, distorted the reality of race relations in the Caribbean.

Subtle suggestions of such sexual fantasies are also present in *Psyche*, H. G. DeLisser's 1959 fictional recreation of Jamaican slave society. Psyche, the novel's beautiful slave protagonist, loses no time in scheming her way into her master's bed. The narrator quickly preempts, at the outset, any misconceptions about the nature of their relationship: "He was still lonely in spite of the companionship of his 'housekeeper,' and this companionship was, after all, erected on a basis of physical attraction only. Psyche was black, and a savage still at heart; he was white and a cultivated man. Besides, the two were entirely different races" (40–41).

In the second configuration of the sexual myth, the woman becomes an object of legitimate violence. Such is the depiction of the *mulata* found in "Mulatta Ballad" ("Copla mulata," 1940), by Puerto Rico's Luis Lloréns Torres:

> This semi-savage half-breed,
> Iberian and Antillean,
> deserves to be driven at full speed
> on the flaming track
> on the Atlantic ocean
> lying between both races.
> This mountain wench,
> who tastes of Jamaican rum,
> greased with hot pepper,
> breathing mustard,
> is on the warm island
> the filly in heat;
> made to be ridden bareback
> up the night's hill till morning,
> fit for staining my silver spurs
> with blood from her flanks. (qtd. in Morales, 42–43)

Sexist discrimination is blatant in both the language and the content of these lines. Unlike the male, the *mulata* is stripped of every vestige of humanity. The image of the filly in heat on whom the rider vents his violent passion effectively animalizes her sexuality. With the sustained animal imagery and the physical violence the male speaker seeks to inflict on her, this poem stands as one of the most undisguised and extreme expressions of male chauvinism and misogyny found in Caribbean literature. Like the prostitute, the *mulata* is the embodiment of Eros ("the filly in heat") and a degraded object of sexual brutality.

This brings to mind that other notion of womanhood, implicitly present here: that of the desexualized (white) angel. The patent sexual contempt that the *mulata* evokes in the speaker seems to be linked to his concept of her racial destiny. He relegates her to a nonhuman category because of her status as a half-breed, seeking in this way to rationalize the sexual violence to be inflicted upon her. She is made into a type of woman on whom it is legitimate for the man to satisfy his perverse and sadistic sexual urges.

Racial prejudice in the speaker is clearly reflected on the surface level of this poem. But the venom transmitted in the vocabulary seems to be a strategy to veil a deeper reality: the profound sexual insecurity that the *mulata* evokes in the speaker. Fantasizing about his sexual domination of her appears to be an attempt to appease these feelings.

Puerto Rican poet Evaristo Ribera Chevremont (1924–1950) also disguises a disquieting reality in "The Black Woman Grinds Her Grain" (La negra muele su grano):

> The black woman grinds her grain
> The black woman, a gentle beast.
> The black woman grinds her grain
> on the wooden table . . .
> Savage is her joy
> When whiteness fills her
> when the white man takes
> her burning black dough. (qtd. in Morales, 54–55)

The bestial connotation ascribed to her expression of sexual ecstasy is all that mitigates the portrait of the woman as an automaton. Reduced to a sexual object, she becomes indistinguishable from the lump of dough she makes. She depends on the white man, specifically and solely, for the experience of sexual satisfaction, for she is a passive vessel that only he can "fill." In this poet's perception she does not feel exploited. On the contrary, she welcomes the white man's favors and is fully gratified by them.

Deeply embedded in this objectification, however, is an ironic reality: the white male speaker depends on the black woman to satisfy his narcissistic desire to prove his sexual potency. Such a view of the legitimacy of the white man's sexual degradation of the Afro-Caribbean woman derives from and expresses the social reality of white group supremacy. While the speaker in the preceding poem shows a psychological need to dehumanize the woman completely, this speaker makes a small concession to her humanity, but only to prove his virility through her sexual response.

White male sexual anxiety also translates into another social anxiety of the white group. In the same way that the "fair lady" is invoked indirectly through the sexualization of her antithesis, the "dark woman," in the relationship between the white man and the black woman, the absent figure is the black man. The white man's sexual dominance in these poems may be seen as another articulation of the discourse of power. It epitomizes both the need of the minority white group in general for social control over blacks and mulattoes, and the specific need of the white man to affirm his domination of the black man through the sexual conquest of the black woman.

Acting as a nexus between the first vision (the woman's sexual dominance) and the second (her sexual objectification) is the disengagement of the white man. In the first instance, there is a complete denial of his personal agency. In the second, his objectification of the woman effectively disavows any emotional involvement on his part. Both perspectives betray a consciousness of the contradiction inherent in the practice of interracial sex in a racist society. These poets constructed this relationship in terms of the white man's "disengaged" involvement with the Afro-Caribbean woman, restricting this interaction to the physical realm. In so doing, they were attempting to maintain the integrity of white supremacist ideology, disavowing the real possibility of sexual attraction occurring naturally between individuals of these two races. Such portrayals of cross-racial sex are, in the main, creations of white male fantasy or, more precisely, the projection of white male desire. They involve some essential elements of the destructive sexual relationships that radical feminists categorize as *thanatica* (from *Thanatos*, the death god in Greek mythology). Noted especially in pornography, thanatic sex is characterized by the inequality of the sexual partners, lack of emotional engagement between them, and sexual interaction based on violence and degradation.

Representations of the sexual relationship between women and men of African descent are rare in Spanish Caribbean literature. Where they occur, however, they typically subvert the white version of interracial sex and display features of the erotic sexual discourse that radical feminists view more favorably. In these cases the participants appear equal in their humanity and identify with each other emotionally. One poem that depicts this type of relationship is "Black Damián, Cane-Cutter" (El negro Damián picador de caña), published by a white female Dominican poet, Colombina de Castellanos. Damián's recollections of his dead lover reveal a deep bond of love:

> Let the drum sing the pain
> of the Negro Damián
> . . . .
> How he loved his black woman
> who filled his coconut cup with love
> and filled his hut with the rhythm

and cadence of her music and song
and filled his life with the breeze of palm leaves!
(qtd. in Morales, 297–98)

The account of their sexual relationship repeats the notion of the black woman's hypersensuality. However, the pleasant associations of the food imagery overshadow the sexual objectification and foreground Damián's appreciation of her sexual value:

And Damián remembers the first night
that he tasted her flesh crisp like fresh sugarcane.
Her smiling face was radiant,

. . . .
her ripe breasts throbbed
her loins were agile
Her open arms like two snakes
coiled around the neck of Damián the Negro
He passed his thirsty lips
over her shiny skin

. . . .
He drank the juice of purple cane
from her body
of ebony beauty. (qtd. in Morales, 298)

Absent from this representation are the violence and the will to dominate noted in the representations of interracial sex. There is also a noticeable semantic difference in the use of similar sexual imagery. The snake metaphor that Muñoz del Monte applies to the *mulata* as a sign of sexual danger takes on here the new connotations of warmth and passion. Reciprocity and engagement between the partners are as much the hallmark of this union as they were missing ingredients in the accounts of interracial sex.

It might be reasonable to associate the difference in sensibility and vision in this poem with the fact that the author is female. But male Afro-Caribbean poets have given a similar tone to their representations. For Jamaican poet George Campbell, writing in 1945, sexual intimacy with the black woman is a pleasurable experience:

Your blackness steeps through me
It wets like dew
It comes upon me like a lovely night
You are not here

Your blackness stays round me like rich perfume
All space black dew.
Your absence beautiful against my loins
Oh! lovely woman like velvet night! (36)

Afro-French Caribbean poets have echoed these sentiments. As early as 1898 Oswald Durand of Haiti declared:

but I shall sing to my black girl
whose mad caress
intoxicates my heart,
I shall offer her verses and songs.
I shall sing of her lip
which never tires,
and which kindles in me passion
and its charming torments. (qtd. in Coulthard, *Race,* 88)

Martinican poet Lionel Attuly exhibits a similar attitude. In "I Write to You from Paris" (Je t'écris de Paris, 1947) he finds in his black woman the sexual pleasure, warmth, and spiritual solace the white woman fails to provide:

I have refound my place in the hollow of your shoulder
on your breast a real breast
capable of supporting the weight of a man's head
of slaking the thirst for peace in a man's heart
for feeding a man's hunger for pleasure
without betrayal. (qtd. in Coulthard, *Race,* 92)

Some male Afro-Caribbean poets assume a more ambiguous posture. Léon Damas, French Guianese *négritude* poet, bored with the "mercenary vendors of love," calls for his black dolls in "Limbé" (1936):

Give me back my black dolls so I can play with them
the naive games of my instinct
remain in the shadow of its laws
recover my courage
my daring
feel myself again
a new self which I was yesterday
without complexities yesterday
at the time of the uprooting. (qtd. in Coulthard, *Race,* 92–93)

The sexual objectification of the woman implied by the image of the black doll, as well as the obvious egocentricity of the speaker's conception of their relationship, are symptoms of the patriarchal design of this discourse. Yet the spiritual and psychological value that the speaker places on the black woman's sexual appeal tempers its undesirable sexist implications. Through his sexual relationship with this woman, the neo-African man can regain the psychic and spiritual wholeness that he lost through deracination. The complementarity of black male and black female is therefore the poem's basic assumption. Rather than the passive plaything that the doll often connotes, the black woman is acknowledged by the black man as his raison d'être, the source of his strength.

A complex interweaving of the discourses of sex, race, and power underlies these representations of sexual interactions. The literary discourses are ultimately transpositions of real social and race relations. While they may be viewed as harmless illusion, they may also function as delusion—as willful distortion of reality.

Miscegenation, Hybridity, and the Nation

Since a rigid stratification was essential for social control during slavery, appropriate legislation was devised to prevent racial mixing and to maintain clear distinctions between blacks and whites. Royal decrees from Spain in 1527 and 1551, for example, stipulated that Negroes marry only Negroes (Mellafe, 117). But the numerous instances of sexual unions between white men and slave women subverted such attempts to prevent miscegenation through legal means. Slave women were often the victims of sexual exploitation. Realizing the benefits derivable from it, however, they soon came to favor sexual union with white men. Through these liaisons they played a notable role in undermining the racial dichotomy on which slave society rested.

Cross-racial intercourse served to transform Caribbean slave society. In the Dominican Republic, for example, in 1650 (forty-eight years after the first slaves were brought to the island) mulattoes formed the largest racial group (Weil et al., 51). They not only represented the failure to maintain discrete racial groupings, but also provoked an ideological crisis in slave society. Certain perceptual and social adjustments had to be made to accommodate them. Though part black, they were also part white and therefore could not be so readily classified with "full-blooded" blacks. Many mulattoes, disavowed by their white fathers, enjoyed no better existence than the black slaves. However, it was also a common practice, especially in the French and Spanish colonies, for fathers to free their mulatto children. These came to form a buffer group between whites and blacks and, together with the group of free blacks, were the precursors of the contemporary Caribbean middle class (E. Williams, *Negro*, 57–59).

Miscegenation has been a prominent subject in Caribbean and Latin American discourse. In 1818 Simón Bolívar, one of the initiators of the struggle for South American independence, declared: "our people . . . are more a mixture of Africa and America than an outcrop of Europe" (qtd. in Beane, 200). Essayists, such as the Argentine Domingo Sarmiento (*Facundo*, 1845) and the Bolivian Alcides Arguedas (*Pueblo enfermo*, 1909), also offered their interpretations of the role of miscegenation in their societies. Their conclusions maintained that *mestizaje* was one of the primary causes of defect in the national psyche and character. Spanish Caribbean writers have created their own version of this theme. Beginning in the nineteenth century they have used the *mulata* to make ideological statements about racial and cultural hybridity. The symbolic values they attach to the African and European ingredients in her racial makeup vary, depending on whether writers assume a Eurocentric or an Afrocentric stance or choose to espouse the intermediate synthetic (Creole) view.

As seen in the preceding chapter, Cuban poets of the nineteenth century were fascinated with the *mulata*. Although there was no unanimity on the question of miscegenation in the society of the time, their portrayals of the *mulata* reveal a remarkable degree of ideological unity. Part of the poets' obsession with this figure stemmed from their view of her hybridity as difference and as deviation from the racial norms of their society. Their work is testimony to the difficulty experienced by the Western-oriented white ruling class in accommodating the *mulata*. She became, in fact, the symbol of a racially divided society unable to conceive of itself as a single nation.

The ideological coherence in these images of the *mulata* manifests itself in a Eurocentric subtext that disparages her African connections. One example is the poem entitled "La mulata," published in 1847 by Cuban poet Creto Gangá (Bartolomé Crespo Borbón). He constructs the *mulata's* racial duality as instability:

She is a blend of everything,
half-pagan and half-Christian,
like her very skin,

half-black, half-white;
like the trout
that wavers between two waters;
a flea that is quiet when it tortures,
but harmless when it jumps;
pepper that pleases the eye
but sets the mouth on fire;
liqueur with soothing smell
and intoxicating effect;
Spanish fly that sometimes vivifies
and sometimes kills. (qtd. in Morales, 310)

The characterization of the *mulata* in the first four lines places her on a nebulous racial midpoint that is both physical (half-black, half-white) and cultural (half-pagan, half-Christian). Her racial character is also constructed as the conjoining of desirable and destructive traits. Underlying the structural symmetry of these lines is a semantic association by which the poet surreptitiously connects the terms in the two paradigms. The *mulata*'s dark color correlates with "pagan" (the sign for aberration), while her white heritage is associated with orthodoxy (Christian). This is the moral-racial pivot around which the subsequent imagery used to describe her revolves. The poet enlarges the view of the *mulata* as the embodiment of duality through the use of images of ambivalence. By means of this oblique strategy, he attributes what he perceives as the *mulata*'s positive characteristics to her European ancestry. Her African heritage, by implication, is responsible for her pernicious qualities.

Not only does the speaker reproduce the ideology that links personality traits to physical appearance, but he also ascribes racial meaning to the color symbolism that associates whiteness with good and blackness with evil. Through the series of analogies between the *mulata* and items with the potential for both good and harm, he construes the black-white mixture as a symbol of ambivalence. Because her complexion confounds the preconceived notion of a dichotomy between black and white, the poet places the *mulata* at an ambiguous point on the metaphorical color spectrum between good and evil. In so doing, he betrays the uncertainty and confusion attending his definition of a figure who defies discrete racial categorization. The potential for wholeness inherent in the opening line fades away in the rest of the poem, a testimony to the fact that, in nineteenth-century Cuban politics, racial plurality inhibited the development of national unity. In fact, as Aline Helg points out, official government policy of the period favored immigration of white families to reduce the proportion of Afro-Cubans in the population (6).

Writing in Cuba in the same period, Francisco Muñoz del Monte also illustrates this preoccupation with the failure to maintain the ideal of racial purity. In "La mulata" the *mulata* becomes not only the embodiment of racial polarization and cultural conflict, but also the vehicle for expressing the poet's belief in the impossibility of racial harmony:

> engendered by two antipathetic beings
> colored by two different princes . . .
> A crossing point between two races
> discordant, implacable, rancorous
> She is claimed by the Caucasians
> She is claimed by the desert.
> Barbarism and civilization wrestle
> in her majestic brown brow
> as on Lucifer's brow one day
> good struggled with evil in Heaven.
> Inexplicable offspring of black and white,
> sublime one, she falls in love at will
> insatiable in anger like the tiger,
> peaceful in love like a dove. (qtd. in Morales, 196–97)

Here the terms that constitute the *mulata's* image emphasize the perceived antithesis of the two worlds from which she is created and the perceived antagonism between them. This is very evident in the invocation of the old civilization-barbarism dichotomy and the assortment of adjectives of disharmony applied to her character. It is a perspective that denies the possibility of wholeness or harmony in a racially mixed individual and, by extension, in a racially mixed society.

Such an opposition to miscegenation is rooted in the ideology that sought to maintain the society's power structure. The *mulata* defied the racist logic of this society that had envisaged no possible rapprochement between white and its alleged racial and social polar opposite, black. Hence she is cast as the "inexplicable" offspring of black and white. Through this mythification the speaker betrays his adherence to the prevailing ideology in the face of the conflicting reality. For a brief moment he admits an alternate view of the *mulata* as the metaphorical bridge spanning the gulf between the two races ("crossing point between two races"). But this possibility dissipates almost immediately in the face of the predominant emphasis on conflict. Since the *mulata* cannot fit into the poet's ideological system as a coherent whole, he can only portray her as the embodiment of unresolved and, perhaps, unresolvable racial conflict.

Muñoz del Monte's portrayal also preserves the binary opposition of white and nonwhite. The speaker's Eurocentric perception of the *mulata* is hardly separable from his prejudice against the African culture she partly represents. In keeping with the stereotype of African barbarism and savagery, he associates the *mulata* elsewhere in the poem with animals that are conventionally depicted as noxious and predatory ("tiger," "lion," "snake"). Devaluation of her African connection is also implicit in the choice of vocabulary; while her European origins are designated in human terms ("Caucasian"), her African origins are reified in a presumed allusion to sub-Saharan Africa ("the desert"). Moreover, the parallel with Lucifer adds a moral dimension to the racial portrait, linking her evil nature to her African heritage. This poet's choice of the *mulata* as a literary subject attests to his recognition of the emerging social force she symbolized. Yet his depiction retains the old racist values used to discriminate against people of African descent.

In the ideological climate of the postcolonial era, many writers have repudiated the notion that ambivalence and conflict are the essence of hybridity. By the early decades of the twentieth century, the more optimistic discourse of creolization had begun to displace the nineteenth-century interpretation of miscegenation. Promotion of the concept of creolization was part of a nationalist effort to revise the interpretation of the racial heterogeneity of Caribbean societies. Creolization places emphasis on the interactive process by which the original encounter of Africa and Europe has produced a hybrid race and culture. Caribbean scholars use the term to refer to "the evolution of a native born-and-bred culture pattern with its own inner logic and consistency different from the feeder sources" (Nettleford, 10). The term *Creole*, used originally to designate a white Caribbean native of European extraction, came to be applied to the mulatto viewed as "new," indigenous, and authentically Caribbean. The nationalist movement that produced *negrismo* and crystallized the sensual stereotype of the Afro-Caribbean woman also engendered the image of the *mulata* as the preeminent Creole symbol.

In response to the nation-building imperative, a dominant trend emerged in Puerto Rican poetry of the 1920s and 1930s: the celebration of the African-European encounter as felicitous and mutual assimilation.

Consequently, poets have romanticized the *mulata*'s racial duality, making her into a symbol of racial integration and national harmony. This is the view promoted by Fortunato Vizcarrondo in the following poem:

Women, black women,
Men of Caucasian race,
Today in my veins circulates
The blood of your races.
I am not white, I am not black,
But, I am proud
to know that I come from Europe
And that I originate in Africa.
But if I cannot be
A black woman, nor a white woman,
Then, something
Must I be with this crossing of races.
I am, with this mixed blood,
A new breed of woman: the Mulatto woman,
Fifty per cent black,
Fifty per cent white.
Blessed, black woman, blessed
Was your love for the white man,
For out of the union
Came the mulatto woman
A mixture that is stronger
Than your race and the Caucasian. (qtd. in Morales, 58)

Although the writer of this poem is male, the voice that speaks is that of the *mulata*, a strategy rarely found in other male poets, for whom she is, typically, a voiceless symbol. Nevertheless, the ideological intention is similar to that found in other postcolonial male poets.

As the ideological imperative becomes dominant, the discourse shifts from concrete description to a symbolic and rhetorical mode. One function of the poem is to reshape the *mulata*'s nineteenth-century image by construing her duality as perfect ethno-racial fusion and equilibrium. In representing herself as the product of the interaction of Africa and Europe, the *mulata* ascribes superiority to neither of her racial constituents, but to the new and discrete type they have produced. Thus, the poet avoids the earlier discrimination against the African side of her heritage through the use of terms with mere referential value, such as "black women" and "men of

Caucasian race." The statement "something / Must I be with this crossing of races" is an affirmation that again collides with the former notion of *mulatez* as an unstable and precarious identity.

In contrast to the consistency evident in the poetry of the nineteenth century, different ideologies compete in the twentieth-century discourses on miscegenation. It is possible to find vestiges of racist ideology more extreme than what the earlier period produced. The durability of the Eurocentric view is evident in the racial disparagement of the *mulata* in Luis Lloréns Torres's "Mulatta Ballad" (Copla mulata), written in 1940:

> This black-haired, black-eyed
> red-mouthed, white-toothed Creole gal;
> . . . .
> This semi-savage half-breed,
> Iberian and Antillean. (qtd. in Morales, 42)

In these lines the deprecatory connotations of the references to her racial hybridity ("semi-savage half-breed") are the center around which the speaker's perception of the *mulata* revolves. Even the ostensibly neutral descriptive epithets—"black-haired," "black-eyed," "red-mouthed," and "white-toothed"—seem to attract the negative value of these racial references. Such an attitude is an anachronistic residue of the initial prejudice directed by whites against the mulatto class because of its African taint.

Other Caribbean writers have been concerned with the issue of the mulatto's racial and ethnic heritage. A notable contemporary example is the St. Lucian Nobel laureate, Derek Walcott, who, like Vizcarrondo, prefers to define the racially mixed individual in essential rather than derivative terms. His "divided," tortured child in *Another Life* confesses:

> But I tired of your whining, grandfather,
> in the whispers of marsh grass,
> I tired of your groans, grandfather,
> in the deep ground bass of the combers. (67)

These lines are the poetic restatement of Walcott's declaration that "mongrel as I am, something prickles in me when I see the word Ashanti as with the word Warwickshire, both separately intimating my grandfathers' roots, both baptizing this neither proud nor ashamed bastard, this hybrid, this West Indian" (qtd. in King, 144). For Walcott, racial identity is a given; it is a matter of neither pride nor shame, for both pride and shame are feelings that imply a view of racial identity as less than natural. In the Francophone areas, however, the mulatto woman is rarely used as a symbol of the merging of the African and European heritage to produce a Caribbean identity, although in Haitian society the preferred female type is the mulatto.

For the *mulata* in the Spanish territories, the discourse of creolization and national integration has provided an alternative to the previously discussed sexualized images and has even served to distinguish her from the black woman. An interesting case of differential treatment of the two is provided by Puerto Rican poet Evaristo Ribera Chevremont, who wrote during the *negrista* period. In "The Black Woman Grinds Her Grain" (La negra muele su grano), discussed earlier, the speaker's insistence on the black woman's animal-like docility is relentless. The line "The black woman, a gentle beast" in the second stanza is repeated in the final stanza, thus giving a definitive quality to her portrait. Chevremont uses a very different strategy in his portrayal of the *mulata* in "Brown Girl" (Morena). While the first poem creates the illusion of realistic portraiture by focusing on the black woman in a typical, concrete work situation, the second offers a romantic and more abstract image that shows no perception of conflict or dichotomy in the *mulata*'s duality:

> You are a brown girl, and your blood
> is purple sugar in the pipes of your veins.
> In your hands—burnished cups—
> are the sands of Mogreb, the roses of Iberia.
> From Spain to the Archipelago, your fathers
> boil their salt in an Andalusian wake.
> Peninsular and Caribbean waters
> discover your beauty in their shells. (qtd. in Morales, 49–50)

A vision of racial confluence and compatibility is evoked by the metaphor of the "Peninsular [Spanish] and Caribbean waters," which is a particularly effective means of articulating an integrationist version of national identity. In addition, in the first two lines the poet exploits the morphological and etymological relationship between the Spanish "caño" (pipe) and the implied "caña" (sugarcane) to associate the *mulata*'s blood with sugar, thereby creating a close identification between her and a typical Caribbean product.

In the rest of the poem he idealizes the *mulata*'s sensuality:

But the grace of your body is unique
unique the fire that burns in your flesh

. . . .

From ears of corn is your flesh made
your unmistakable brown girl flesh

. . . .

I taste in the Antillean honeycombs
the sweet honey of your tongue
The sweetness that you have in your lips
is lacked by women of other lands. (qtd. in Morales, 50–51)

Although the speaker reproduces the stereotype of the sensual *mulata,* he has also modified it by not characterizing this sensuality as threatening or destructive. He associates it instead with nature's productive forces. For him it is this creative sensuality that defines Caribbeanness ("lo antillano").

Other poets evoke the *mulata*-Creole image less directly, through a similar Caribbeanization of the discourse. For example, Emilio Ballagas's "Cuba, Poetry" (Cuba, poesía) is a patriotic celebration of "lo cubano." The poem is replete with typical images of Cuban reality and incorporates the *mulata* as an implicit cultural and racial symbol:

For me the stem of the guitar
is slender like a mulatto girl.

. . . .

I have felt next to me the throb
of mixed flesh
my hands have slid softly
over skin the color of naseberry
and the sun rose in a sensual mouth
to kiss me. *(Elegía,* 12)

In like fashion, Dominican poet Manuel del Cabral associates the *mulata* with typical musical instruments:

In the swaying of the hammock
you rock your maracas laughter
as if you suddenly created the dawn
in your drumskin body. (qtd. in Morales, 221)

This appropriation of the *mulata* as a cultural symbol finds even more elaborate expression in "Mulata-Antilla," the famous 1937 poem of Puerto Rico's Luis Palés Matos:

In you now, mulatto girl,
I take refuge in the warm Caribbean sea.
Slow sensual water of molasses
sugar port, warm bay,
with light at rest
gilding the clear waves,
and the sleepy bee-hive buzz
of people bustling on the shore
. . . .
In you now, mulatto girl . . .
Oh what a wonderful awakening in the Caribbean
wild color that hits the high notes,
Red-hot music of joy
and burning goads of perfume
—lime, tobacco, pineapple—
their voices drunk with delight
enticing the senses.
Now you are, mulatto girl,
the whole sea and land of my islands.
A symphony of fruits whose notes burst forth
furiously in the perfume of your body
. . . .
in your womb my two races blend
their vital expansive powers. (qtd. in Morales, 81–82)

As imaged here, the *mulata* has retained the essence but not the grossness
of the rumba dancer's sensuality. The poet links her sensuality less to
erotic body signs and more to the pleasing sights, smells, products, and
sensations of the natural world. This representation of sensuality signals
a recuperation of that bourgeois discourse against which the earlier
negrista poets had rebelled. It is in concert with the social position of both
the *mulata* and the creator of her image. Although the poem repeats the
notion of racial harmony, the identification of the *mulata* with the more
neutral natural phenomena effectively displaces race as the central concept
that defines nationality.

Personification of the land as a woman is one of the most enduring of
literary conventions. In early literary and artistic representations of the
European conquest of America, the Caribbean appears as a native woman
who in her primitive and passive state is conquered and colonized by a
superior European male. In continuing the tradition of feminizing the

land, Caribbean writers of the twentieth century have displaced the supine image by casting the nation in the form of a defiant mulatto woman. Jamaican poet W. Adolphe Roberts develops the nationalist image in "The Maroon Girl" (1949), where he identifies his Maroon girl, with her "blood of white and black," with the flora of the land and presents her as a symbol of national resistance:

> She is a peasant, yet she is a queen.
> She is Jamaica poised against attack.
> Her woods are hung with orchids; the still flame
> Of red hibiscus lights her path, and starred
> With orange and coffee blossoms is her yard.
> She stands on ground for which her fathers died;
> Figure of savage beauty, figure of pride. (qtd. in Coulthard, *Race*,
>   93)

Strategies such as these have been integral to the enterprise of decolonization and the growth of an indigenous cultural tradition, which followed upon the gaining of political independence. The deepening of antiimperialist sentiments in the Caribbean in the 1930s gave added impetus to this movement.

In Puerto Rico the struggle against U.S. domination assumed violent proportions in the nationalist revolt that was suppressed in the 1935 Massacre of Río Piedras. Poems that use the *mulata* as a Creole icon reflect this political development. In Evaristo Chevremont's "Brown Girl" (Morena), she becomes an icon of the nation, and the act of representation itself becomes a rhetorical defense of the nation against the imperialist designs of external powers:

> Perchance the foam of pirates besieges,
> with jealous bubbles, the beaches,
> where, ripened by your warmth, you surrender
> your wealth to the desires of your lover
>
> . . . .
> And I, guardian of your riches
> in flesh and blood, avidly guard,
> your silhouette in fine lockets. (qtd. in Morales, 51)

The *mulata* in "The Shake It Song" (Plena del menéalo), another 1937 poem by Luis Palés Matos, symbolizes the forces of resistance to, and salvation from, neocolonialist domination:

In the rushing movement
your skirt unfurls
like a sail in the wind;
your buttocks are the helm
and your breasts the stem;
on we go, weather vane of the sea,
to meet the cyclone,
for on your skillful sailing
depends your salvation.
Dance on! . . .
Hold on to the stern, while you dance;
that dance will save you from
the monsieur who waits
across the sea.
Shake your smooth belly
sweetened in the canefields . . .
While you dance, no one dares
change your heart or change the salt.
No *agapitos* here,
No misters there.
Hold on to the stern, mulatta
Keep rolling your hips
into eternity
for it is the gust of a hurricane,
and shake it, shake it!
This way and that way, that way and this way
shake it, shake it
till Uncle Sam goes mad! (Palés Matos, 181–83)

A new political significance marks the sensuality of the dancing *mulata*. Her dancing symbolizes that which is authentically Puerto Rican and therefore more enduring than the American (místeres) and the American-ized (agapitos).

These poems illustrate well the observation made by Richard Jackson that in their attempt to create an original Latin American culture, the "select minority" of Latin American writers have recognized that origi-nality has to be sought in the nonwhite racial groups ("Literary," 5). The poets made the *mulata* into a symbol to encapsulate both the concrete and the intangible aspects of national life. By making her into an idealized abstraction, they sought, not to achieve historical accuracy, but to promulgate a national myth. The *mulata* was a racially expedient figure, who could synthesize the African and European constituents of their nation and serve as an emblem in whom both ethnic groups could recognize themselves and relate to each other. At the same time, such representations were, in part, a preemptive gesture. They were designed to ward off the perceived danger of overemphasis on the African element of Caribbean culture, which would lead to the exclusion of whites.

This dissemination of a symbol of a hybrid national identity is similar to the frequent use of slogans such as "out of many, one people" in other racially heterogeneous Caribbean societies. R. T. Smith's comment that such slogans evade but do not erase ethnic differences is relevant to the situation of the Spanish Caribbean, where the use of the *mulata* is a rhetorical solution to a political problem (54). Claims that racial unity is a societal norm are now a common part of postcolonial Caribbean rhetoric. Throughout the real Caribbean, however, and in the Spanish-speaking territories in particular, racial integration continues to be an illusive dream. The "negrification" of the *mulata* by some poets offers an alternative to the integrationist stereotype.

"Bronze Philosophy" (Filosofía de bronce), published in 1929 by Cuban poet Felipe Pichardo Moya, is a reminder of the course of historical events that bred the *mulata*:

Of your ancestors you retain
God knows how many!
How many unknown pedigrees
that form your present being!

Savage blood, and our blood
mixed beneath a compliant sun
with the blessing of a sinister hand,
they are the light in your eyes!

. . . .

Oh, the noble Spanish grandfather,
yielded to the impulse stirred in him
by the black flesh of the slave
one siesta drunk with the sun!
Monstrous idyll among the cane cuttings,
illicit conception

. . . .

And in a copy of the horrors of hell
forever without equal,
perhaps the seed of your father
felt the lashes on the torso of your mother!

And so you came to us,
our sister and their sister,
supreme flower of injustice,
who converts into wild stallions
the doves of a caress
in vengeful desire
kept alive in your haunches,
because your passionate impulse
elevates, above the embrace,
the fury of the lashes
of the merciless overseer! (qtd. in Morales, 325–26)

Since the nineteenth century, bronze had become a standard literary metaphor for the *mulata's* skin color and her hybrid makeup. In spite of the expectations raised by its use in this title, however, the poem places greater emphasis on the *mulata's* black origins than on her racial duality. In the opening lines the reference to her "unknown pedigrees" serves as a corrective to the conventional disparagement of her African heritage. At the same time, the poet invokes the sexual exploitation of the slave woman to undercut the characterization of her Spanish forebear as noble. From this perspective, not only is the *mulata* linked more closely to the world of her black mother, but miscegenation, which she symbolizes, is construed as a form of mongrelization of the African pedigree. This rejection of the European heritage and the more favorable association of the *mulata* with an African past is atypical in the Hispanic Caribbean tradition and is more in concert with the ideology of French *négritude*. Pichardo Moya's stance might, however, have also stemmed from the residual anti-Spanish sentiment that persisted in Cuba long after that country had gained political independence.

This poet resists the facile signification imposed on the *mulata* by those earlier poets who had marginalized history in representing her as an emblem of racial and cultural integration. Their insistence on the *mulata* as product had merely obscured the process by which she was frequently conceived. By giving a diachronic dimension to his account, Pichardo Moya places miscegenation in the context of the slavery in which it occurred. He does not portray the African-European encounter out of which she was born as a happy union, but uses the *mulata* primarily to evoke the violence that the Spanish slave master inflicted on the African slave. Although the dialectic of the civilized Self and the barbaric Other is reproduced here ("savage blood and our blood"), its function is ironic, for there is an implicit reverse application of the term "savage," which, in this context, clearly characterizes the actions of the white overlord.

In addition, any suggestion that the *mulata* is a symbol of national integration is overshadowed by an accentuation of the cruelties and injustice of the slave past. Irony is the strategy used for this purpose. For example, the juxtaposition of disparate terms in the phrase "monstrous idyll" functions as a refutation of the notion of miscegenation as natural assimilation. And the bitter ironic twist in the line "supreme flower of injustice" further preempts the possibility of celebration of the *mulata* as a unifying symbol.

The pain of the slave woman in this account is not the pain of sexual ecstasy in other versions of interracial sexual encounters; it is the real pain of the physical brutality often inflicted upon her and her kind. Through the shocking image of the beating of the slave woman even while she carries her master's child in her womb, the speaker forges a vicarious link between the *mulata* and the suffering of her mother. Nor does the poet pretend that the *mulata* symbolizes the present resolution of the racial antagonism created by slavery. In a cynical stroke, the last lines of the final stanza translate the myth of the sexually threatening *mulata* into an expression of the continuing desire to avenge past injustice.

In a reference to the identity of Jamaican mulattoes, Rex Nettleford observes that "they have been reared for the most part more as their *Black* mothers' offsprings and less as their *White* fathers' children" (9). The image of the *mulata* projected in "Black Roots" (Raíz negra, 1942), by Puerto Rican poet Marigloria Palma, suggests such an Afrocentric definition of creolization. Palma allows the *mulata* to express both her perception of her own identity and how she wants to be perceived:

> I am a cross between a heron and a jet-black crow,
> My corn was suckled by ebony breasts,
> Then spread its wings out to the white lemon tree
> There was a crossing of soot and boiling milk
> and a sprouting of wild-haired mulattoes.
> . . . .

In me blackness roars with its stronger tones

. . . .

My blood runs through me like a nest of black ants
crying in the poison of my purple graft
Jet-black are my thoughts and feelings; cinnamon the color of my
    skin. (qtd. in Morales, 159–60)

The discourse functions on two levels to affirm the *mulata's* identity. While she defines her biological identity in terms of hybridization ("a cross between a heron and a jet-black crow"), her cultural and psychic identities inhere in her matrilinear black origins ("My corn was suckled by ebony breasts"; "Jet-black are my thoughts and feelings").

In "Yelidá" (1942), Tomás Hernández Franco uses another strategy to link the mulatto woman with her black heritage. Like his compatriot and predecessor Francisco Muñoz del Monte, this poet invokes the conflict between "civilization" and "barbarism" as a paradigm in his representation of racial mixing. The mythic struggle between the "terrible" voodoo gods of African origin and the weaker European gods who have come to the Caribbean to rescue the white blood in Yelidá (the mulatto offspring of the Norwegian Erick and the black Haitian Madam Suquí) ends with the triumph of the African-derived gods. Yelidá, the *mulata,* thus embodies a national identity defined less by its duality and more by the dominance of the African-oriented culture. But because of the unfavorable associations evoked by the allusions to the *mulata's* African heritage, the portrait reflects a Eurocentric vision similar to that of Muñoz del Monte's. The triumph of the voodoo gods signifies implicitly the ascendancy of barbarism. But while Muñoz del Monte may be seen to be reproducing the discourse of his nineteenth-century world, the prejudice against the African heritage shown by Hernández Franco is an anachronism. When he published this poem in 1942, the revisionist efforts of Caribbean intellectuals, politicians, and artists were producing more positive interpretations of racial mixing.

In their meditations on miscegenation, Spanish Caribbean poets have used the *mulata* to reflect on the racial interaction in colonial society and to imply the resolution of the racial problem inherited from that past. In fact, they show their complicity with the official claim that racial integration is the societal norm in the Caribbean. However, some studies of race relations have questioned this assumption. Sociologist H. Hoetink has noted that the appearance of friendliness between the various racial groups in the Spanish Caribbean is often artificial and superficial (22). Thomas Matthews corroborates this view in his observation that in Puerto Rico "racial discrimination does not appear openly in public places or governmental circles, but operates mostly in the social and private spheres of activity" (314). According to Hoetink, the findings of O. Noguiera regarding race relations in Brazil also apply to the Caribbean, where appearance (skin color and other physical features) is a strong basis of racial prejudice (53). Of Puerto Rico he notes that the less pronounced the Negroid features of an individual, the greater the chances of social acceptance, and he adds that "some of the most prominent Puerto Ricans have Negro ancestors, but their own prosperity and the fact that they themselves look white are decisive elements in their upper-class position" (39). Exaltations of *mulatez* as the symbol of Caribbean culture and of racial and national integration thus disseminate as reality what, in effect, is desire. Other writers have sought to correct the erroneous equation of symbolic gestures and superficial cultural gains with real social achievement.

3

From Voiceless Object to Human Subject
Filling the Historical Vacuum

In promoting their fanciful images of black and mulatto women as aesthetic objects and erotic bodies, many of the (mainly male) writers have been concerned with challenging traditional representations. In the process they have ignored the sociohistorical and human contexts of the lives of their literary subjects. They have substituted stereotypes and abstractions for reality and have embraced the more rhetorical modes of representation. Competing with these representational practices is the approach of other writers who have focused on the Afro-Caribbean woman's lived reality and have shed light on the often obscured and more disturbing human and social dimensions of her experience. These counterimages do not all correspond to a specific historical time or literary moment, but are expressions of an ongoing challenge to the authority of the dominant discourses and ideologies. Their function has been to deromanticize and demythify the entrenched representations.

The Black Matriarch in the Closet

The fact that initially the black woman, rather than the black man, was the usual agent of miscegenation has created a unique role for her in considerations of identity in the Spanish Caribbean. For mixed-race individuals who seek to identify with their white origins, the black female forebear becomes a negative symbol—the embodiment of the shameful half of their racial heritage. In "Black behind the Ears" (El negro tras de la oreja), a poem published in 1883, the Dominican Juan Antonio Alix uses the figure of the black grandmother to satirize the pretentious posture of such individuals:

The white man whose grandmother
Was as black as coal,
Of her never makes mention
Though they may set him on fire,
But as for his aunt White Bean,
Who was an old white lady
He never fails to mention her,
Just to make believe,
That he could never be
"Black behind the ears." (qtd. in Morales, 202)

The theme reappears in the popular poem "And Your Grandmother, Where Is She?" (¿Y tu agüela, a'onde ejtá?), published in 1942 by Puerto Rican Fortunato Vizcarrondo. He portrays the "invisible" black grandmother as an emblem of the pervasive but frequently denied black racial heritage of Puerto Ricans:

Yesterday you called me nigger
Today I'll give my reply:
My mother sits in the living room,
And your grandmother, where is she?

My hair is coarse like hemp rope;
Yours is just like silk;
Your father's is very straight,
And your grandmother, where is she?

Your color turned out white
your cheeks they are pink;
your lips are thin . . .
And your grandmama, where is she?

. . . .

But I know her too well!
They call her Miss Tatá . . .
You hide her in the kitchen
For she is black in truth. (qtd. in Morales, 56–57)

An equivalent of the black female emblem can also be found in the poetry of the English-speaking Caribbean. Eric Roach of Trinidad and Tobago refers scathingly to this black racial shame in "Letter to Lamming in England" (1952):

We are enslaved in the ancestral cane,
We're trapped in our inheritance of lust,
The brown boot scorns the black,
And skins not white as white
Deny the black old matriarch in the cupboard. (qtd. in Baugh, 12)

These poems highlight the lingering problems of miscegenation that undermine attempts to forge national unity.

The role of the black matriarch is the subject of a less known poem entitled "La mulata" written by Fortunato Vizcarrondo. Like the Cuban Nicolás Guillén in his "Ballad of Two Grandfathers" (Balada de los dos abuelos), Vizcarrondo is promoting an integrationist ideology. He assigns the black matriarch a positive role in the shaping of racial identity:

Because of one, because of one black woman
The white race became tainted
. . . .
Because of one beautiful black woman
Aristocracy was lost
Oh powerful, so powerful
Was the love of an African woman!
. . . .
Oh powerful, so powerful
Was the love of an African woman
And the daring sensuality
That conquered aristocracy! (qtd. in Morales, 58–59)

Vizcarrondo's allusion to the beautiful black woman who not only seduced but also inspired love in the white male "aristocrat" effectively inverts the other image of the black female forebear as a shameful signifier. In addition, the poem proposes an alternative to the representation of the African slave woman as victim of the white overlord's sexual exploitation. Through the deliberate semantic ambiguity and irony in the phrases "because of one black woman" and "the love of an African woman," the poet invites the reader to view the black woman simultaneously as the reason for, and the agent of, racial cross-fertilization. In Vizcarrondo's view, she undermined the aristocratic pretensions of the ruling class and was an active coparticipant with the white male in the miscegenation process.

Some Haitian poetry expresses a version of Vizcarrondo's vision. As noted by Hoffmann, it is the black woman, rooted in an African past, who is seen to represent the nation:

> And listening to your song, Grandmother,
> I understood, in my soul and my blood
> That the roots of your life
> Still tied you to stricken Africa. (qtd. in Hoffmann, 96)

Or she becomes the incarnation of Africa in the Caribbean: "Africa in flesh and blood" (Hoffmann, 96).

Psychosocial Dilemmas

Representations of the *mulata* that reduce her to her aesthetic and sexual attributes and those that constitute her as the symbol of the nation have effaced many aspects of her problematic past and painful present. The emergence of the mulatto class, and with it a more nuanced color spectrum, left basically unchanged the white racial bias of slave society. It also created disunity between mulattoes and blacks. As Eric Williams has noted, the intermediate mulatto caste in slave society despised the black side of its ancestry: "With the prestige of white blood in their veins, they refused to do laboring work. They despised the 'no-good niggers'" (*Negro*, 58). At the center of this conflict was the mulatto woman, who, in her capacity as the white man's concubine, frequently acted as informer against the field slaves. Her relative superiority to the black woman was partial compensation for the mulatto woman's status as the white woman's inferior.

Colonial Cuban writers in general submerged this discomfiting truth beneath their fixation with the *mulata*'s physical beauty and racial hybridity. In Antonio Zambrana's *El negro Francisco* (1873), for example, although realism prevails in those episodes that depict the horrors of slavery, the account of the beautiful *mulata* Camila's love for the black slave Francisco is more attentive to the demands of a Romantic love story than to the racial politics of slave society. Only the shattering of her illusion of being accepted as part of the white world leads Camila to fall in love with Francisco. Through this incredibly unproblematic process she claims her black heritage.

On the other hand, Juan Antonio Alix, a white poet writing in the Dominican Republic in the late nineteenth century, offers a more candid view of the *mulata* in "A Colored Woman Who Rejects Her Companion for a White Man" (Una mujer de color que desprecia a un compañero suyo por blanco):

This advice I give you
because I really care,
Never deny your race
For the black man is your true mate
If the white man's love you crave
Your own race do not despise
For there is no white man to love you
Like a man of your own race. (qtd. in Morales, 203)

In its historical context Alix's poem appears to be an objective and revolutionary comment on the *mulata*'s role in promoting racial conflict. Implicitly it censures her for internalizing that society's white supremacist values and for rejecting her black heritage. But also underlying his reproach are the speaker's own covertly racist motives. When he declares that the black man is her natural partner, he speaks less out of altruistic concern and more out of a desire to ensure that the *mulata* remain in her assigned place and not aspire to social advancement through an alliance with a white man. Alix's ostensible disinterest therefore translates into an active, though subtle, endorsement of the practice of racial segregation. It is an attempt to safeguard the interests of his own race and class.

Forty years later, in 1930, Cuban literature still places a version of this recalcitrant *mulata* figure at the center of racial tensions and antagonisms. The black male speaker in Nicolás Guillén's "La mulata" deflates her for demonstrating antiblack prejudice:

They tell me, mulatto girl,
mulatto girl, now I know you say
I have a nose like the knot in a tie.

But listen to what I tell you
You are not much better off
for you have a real big mouth
and your nappy hair is red
. . . .
But if you only knew the truth, mulatto girl,
With my black girl I have enough
and I don't need you at all! (I:104)

Guillén is concerned here with lived reality rather than with literary rhetoric. Rejecting the perspective of the nationalists who had turned the *mulata* into an empty symbol, he illustrates instead, through her racist stance, the very real psychological obstacles that impede the development of national unity. Guillén's *mulata* exhibits an aversion to blackness that translates into a fear of her own racial heritage. At the same time, the despised black suitor's declared preference for his black woman comes only after the *mulata* has rejected him. His affirmation merely upholds the black woman's subaltern status.

In *The Black Image in the White Mind*, George Fredrickson points to the large role played by the visibility of racial difference in perpetuating the prejudice against people of African descent: "slavery had been reserved for men of a different color, and this conjunction of servitude and color, which made the ex-slave readily and permanently identifiable, had planted the seeds of disaster by creating a problem of race more fundamental and difficult to solve than the problem of slavery" (23). One can hardly overemphasize the long-lasting and detrimental psychological consequences of this original racial situation for the large numbers of Caribbean people whose origins can be traced back to the black slaves.

This psychological encumbrance is the subject of *Black Skin, White Masks* (1952), Martinican psychiatrist Frantz Fanon's seminal work on race in the colonial experience. Fanon recognized the important role literature plays in the conveyance of social values. Hence, although he supported his theses through case-study observation of attitudes and behavior, he often turned to analysis of literary texts featuring black and brown characters for illustrations of the malaise. The white mask in Fanon's study is a metaphor for the mental colonization from which people of African descent have suffered historically, the persistent self-doubt, self-hate, and feelings of inferiority resulting from their complete dependence on others for their self-image.

Some Spanish Caribbean writers have given prominence to this experience of alienation. It is prominent in the work of Carmen Colón Pellot, a female Puerto Rican poet. In 1938 Colón Pellot published a short collection of poems under the title *Ambar mulato*, in which she problematizes the *mulata* image. She explores the psychic dilemma of a notionally "real" mulatto woman and challenges the preceding notions that she is the unequivocal beneficiary of her proximity to the white female model. Her *mulata* does not rest confidently on her superiority over blacks. One poem's title, "Oh Lord, I Want to Be White" (¡Ay, señor, que yo quiero ser blanca!), is the cry of a *mulata* in the throes of a crisis of racial identity:

On the steep, shy
virgin slopes of the mountains,

the orange tree bears blossoms
with goodness perfumed.

In their untainted beauty
and their pure whiteness,
my fingers do not break them
nor my voice stain them.

Oh, my Jesus!
Oh Lord, I want to be white!
The pond of water revels
In its green birth
for the stars converse
in its clear brightness.

It shows no sign of the poppy
that is in my scarlet dream;
my songs do not taint it
the mud does not disturb it.

Oh, my Jesus!
Oh Lord, I want to be white!

The waves unfurl
their foamy crests on the beach;
in innocent playfulness,
rising, falling.

The sea has its mantilla
and I have my guitar;
the sea is decked as a bride,
I am dressed in scarlet.

Oh, my Jesus!
Oh Lord, I want to be
blond and white:
like the foam,
like the pond,
like the blossoms
of the orange trees
on my mountain. (qtd. in Morales 149–50)

The poet's choice of a first-person discourse allows her to personalize the *mulata*'s plight and to lay bare, more convincingly, the discrepancy between literary stereotype and lived reality. Her *mulata* exhibits the other side of the fear of being black expressed by Guillén's *mulata:* the yearning to be white. Although the concept of whiteness is embodied euphemistically in images from the natural environment (orange blossoms, foam, pond), what the *mulata* hankers after is the white woman's beauty; she wants to be white and blond. Her inferiority complex is mirrored even in the arrangement of ideas in the poem, much of which gives priority to the elaboration of images of whiteness, thereby indicating its status as the aesthetic ideal.

This poem is a tragic illustration of one psychic consequence of the dominance of white aesthetic standards. Self-alienation results from the *mulata*'s obsession with an inaccessible whiteness. Not only does the use of a private voice making supplication to God heighten the intensity of her desire, but the obvious futility of her quest seals her tragedy. In defining herself, the *mulata* persona also makes use of the language of Christian morality, which attaches spiritual values to color. She desires whiteness not only as a physical ideal, but also for its association with virtue and chastity. Hence she characterizes white beauty as "unpolluted" and "immaculate" and attributes qualities such as virginity and sanctity to whiteness. Obliquely, the *mulata* portrays herself as the negation of purity, as that which tarnishes and defiles. Her self-image depends totally on her perception of her white counterpart. She has internalized that perception of race that has led to the aesthetic, sexual, and moral devaluation of the colored woman. Thus, the desire to be white is also accompanied by the desire to escape the stigma of sinful sex traditionally associated with her black taint (represented in the allusion to the prostitute, the proverbial "scarlet woman").

In another poem from the same collection and with an equally explicit title, "Roots of *Mulata* Envy" (Motivos de envidia mulata), Colón Pellot highlights the link between the *mulata*'s race and her social status:

> I envy you,
> white cloud;
> you fall in love in the arms
> of the wind;
> you alone can move
> among the virile trees
> of the high mountains;
> they pay tribute to you
> for your chastity and beauty.

No one praises me in song;
norms, Christian laws
enslave me.

The sky smiles on you;
space pampers and regales you
you give all to the sun, as you fancy,
voluptuous and vague,
amid the shining kisses
and the caresses of the rainbowed light.

No one seeks my brown smiles;
no one worships me,
though I have sap in my
warm, bubbling goblets.
Your color is snowy,
my inheritance is tanned.

While I splash in mud
you are rocked in white;
atop the world,
scorning the lowly swamps.

In the quiet night
the handsome stars
wink at you.
You float, flirtingly
and you rendezvous
with the most handsome
one who seeks your love.

And so, seeing you so free
seeing myself so enslaved,
an old sadness comes over me
and I feel such deep envy
of you, white cloud. (qtd. in Morales, 146–47)

Again the contrapuntal characterization of the *mulata* and her white counterpart forms the poem's structural frame. As in the first poem, the speaker uses the euphemistic image of the cloud to represent the dominance of whiteness. The location of the cloud, like that of the blossoms of the orange tree growing on the mountain in the preceding poem, is a spatial representation of the socio-racial distance between the two women. While the cloud is identified with superior space and its elements—the wind, the sun, the sky, and the stars—the *mulata* identifies with the lowly earth. The earth image does not bear the usual connotations of creativity and fertility but is associated with the pollution and unwholesomeness of mud and swamps.

Colón Pellot's poem highlights the social origins of the *mulata*'s psychological dilemma. The contrast between the acceptance accorded the white woman and the exclusion experienced by the *mulata* foregrounds the correlation between skin color and social status. It is the system of power relations that confers freedom, virtue, and beauty on the white woman and that guarantees her a place, while placing restrictions on the *mulata* because of her black taint. Her representation of her condition as a form of enslavement links this black taint back to the institution of slavery and its supporting ideology, and suggests a continuation of that bondage through the surviving caste system.

But although the speaker's recognition of the injustice of the race-class division implies some measure of protest, she acquiesces to the notion of her own inherent inferiority. Her questioning of the existing racial value system that discriminates against her stems from a desire, not to change the system, but to rise to the dominant position in the racial hierarchy. Both poems illustrate well the process of cultural conditioning whereby her internalization of white supremacist ideology determines the *mulata*'s self-perception. Her desire to be white is self-denying and results in unhappiness. It is one manifestation of a psychological attitude that, in the words of Erna Brodber, "diverts time and mental energy from more creative activities and, most detrimental of all, crystallizes an inferiority complex" (36). These confessions of self-alienation displace the glorified image of the *mulata*-Creole, and demythify the rhetoric of the nationalists who had consecrated her as an inert symbol of racial harmony. Shown as a feeling subject, she does not conform to their rhetorical image.

French Caribbean literature is replete with examples of women novelists who focus primarily on similar manifestations of Afro-Caribbean women's psychic predicament. Successive novels that have appeared since Mayotte Capécia's *Je suis Martiniquaise* in 1948 explore the alienation from self and from society that is the inexorable dilemma of the majority of these novels' female protagonists. Tragedy always stalks these women as their search for psychic wholeness results in apparently inevitable psychic disintegration. Marie Chauvet's *Fille d'Haiti* (1954) and *Amour*

(1960), Michèle Lacrosil's *Sapotille et le Serin d'argile* (1960) and *Cajou* (1961), Maryse Condé's *Heremakhonon* (1976) and *Une Saison à Rihata* (1981), and Myriam Warner-Vieyra's *Le Quimoiseur l'avait dit* (1980) and *Juletane* (1982) are some of the novels that have helped to create this distinct Francophone Caribbean tradition. Their racial identity crisis dogs these mixed-race characters in their Caribbean home and in metropolitan France. Far from relieving their psychic distress, migration to Africa paradoxically heightens their dilemma.

Guadeloupian novelist Myriam Warner-Vieyra explores the plight of one such woman in *Juletane*. In Africa or the French Caribbean, Juletane is an outsider, a "leper." African women in the novel deny her black identity, because of her European acculturation. She, in turn, displays contempt for her African counterparts. Retreat into madness is her only defense. Thus, like Colón Pellot, who tacitly debunks the myth of national integration that the Hispanic *mulata* has been used to symbolize, Warner-Vieyra dispels the *négritude* myth of a paradisiacal African homeland where alienated Afro-Caribbean women can find liberation.

Anglophone Caribbean literature also bears witness to the psychological predicament of the black woman because of the social stigma attached to her racial features. In "Kinky Hair Blues" (1937), Una Marson, a black Jamaican poet, records such a woman's vain effort to resist the power of the dominant white aesthetic ideal:

> Lord 'tis you did gie me
> All dis kinky hair.
> 'Tis you did gie me
> All dis kinky hair,
> And I don't envy gals
> What got dose locks so fair.
> I like me black face
> And me kinky hair
>
> . . . .
> But nobody loves dem,
> I jes don't tink it's fair. (qtd. in Burnett, 158)

Marson places the black woman's self-image problem in its sociogenetic framework. Community expectation hampers her quest for freedom to define herself. Fear of the inevitable isolation that will arise from such a posture of resistance aborts the attempt to maintain racial integrity. Through cosmetic transformation she will make herself less black:

I's gwine press me hair
And bleach me skin.
What won't a gal do
Some kind of man to win. (qtd. in Burnett, 159)

The Sexual Myth Deconstructed

The appearance in 1930 of a short collection of poems, *Motivos de son*, by the Afro-Cuban Nicolás Guillén, is usually considered a watershed in the evolution of Spanish Caribbean poetry on the black experience. It represents one of the earliest efforts to direct literary attention to the everyday lives of the Afro-Cuban population and to provide a corrective to the *negrista* writers' one-dimensional representations and distortions of history. Set in the slums of Havana, the poems capture the spontaneity of the interaction between black and mulatto actors and speakers. Guillén's portrayal of the Afro-Cuban woman as mate and lover of the black man displaces the conventional discourse on sex. In the first place, the sex act and even sexual allusions do not occupy the center of these poems. Sexual intimacy is not treated explicitly but can only be assumed by the reader, for the poet's main concern is the social context in which these relationships develop.

Motivos de son affords the reader a complex, unromanticized, and disturbing view of the love affairs of Afro-Cuban men and women. It highlights, for example, the materialistic considerations that lead the speaker in "Go Get Money" (Búcate plata) to leave her lover because, as she declares, "love without money, man, / no way!" (I:108). However, the words of psychological comfort and affection that Caridá offers her man indicate the existence of another type of relationship based on love:

Why do you get mad
when they call you blubber-lipped Negro
when your mouth is so sweet,
blubber-lipped Negro?
Blubber-lipped Negro the way you are
you have it all:
Caridá supports you,
she gives you it all. (I:103)

In these situations the man views the woman as neither sexual sensation nor sexual threat:

The girl that I have,
as black as she is,
I would not change her
for no other woman.

She knows how to wash, to iron, to sew,
And, man, how that woman can cook!

If they come get her
to go dancing,
or eating,
she's got to take me,
she's got to bring me.

She says: "Daddy boy,
Don't you leave me;
let's go,
let's go,
let's go
have some fun." (I:108–9)

From a feminist viewpoint the speaker may, defensibly, be criticized for seeming to value the woman mainly for her domestic functions. Still, there are intimations of emotional engagement between the two, which was absent from the representations of her relationship with the white man. In the latter accounts, the Afro-Caribbean woman is defined as the Other, or serves to validate the white man's virility. Now Guillén invites the reader to observe her as she views and is viewed by the men of her own ethnic community, usually with no apparent mediation by a third consciousness.

By placing her in her everyday environment, Guillén deconstructs the sexual myth and discloses other sides of the personality that the myth had obscured. *Motivos de son* manifests its iconoclasm not only through the difference in the context and content of the poet's depiction of the relationships between these men and women, but also through the radical discursive transformation that the poems exemplify. Guillén replaces voyeurism with the more direct revelations of the actors themselves. The appropriation of the *son*, a popular musical form, and the use of the linguistic register that approximates Afro-Cuban speech patterns also give a more profound character to Guillén's aesthetic revolt in these poems.

In "When Women Love Men" (Cuando las mujeres quieren a los hombres), from her 1976 short story collection *Papeles de Pandora*, Puerto Rican feminist Rosario Ferré has recourse to a more complex strategy in dismantling the myth of the black woman's sexuality. What distinguishes her representation is her affiliation of Isabel la Negra, the "black wench," with Isabel Luberza, the "white lady." In the established discourses on sexuality, the white stereotype that Ferré releases in her short story had always been present as a subtextual contrast for the dark-skinned woman. Few writers, however, have dealt explicitly with the white woman in this context. Ferré juxtaposes the sexual mystique that has shrouded the woman of African descent with the myth of asexuality that has been woven around the white woman in order to challenge the authority of both stereotypes. Each woman is presented as a creature of the other's fantasy. Each defines herself in relation to the other. Each constructs her own identity and assesses her role by defining and assessing the other. Isabel la Negra has internalized the myth of her sexual superiority over the white woman. In the black mind, white female sexuality is ridiculed; in the white mind, black female sexuality is degraded.

By revealing the pervasiveness of the stereotypes of each woman in Puerto Rican literature, popular culture, and society, the story reminds us of the status of each as representation. Ferré looks beyond the static one-dimensional portraits to find the women behind the myths. She uses their individual voices to present them as full human beings. In contrast to the carefree rumba dancer of *negrismo*, Isabel la Negra appears, on the one hand, as the victim of sexual exploitation by rich white or Latino men. On the other, she constructs an image of herself as a sexual agent, the provider of an indispensable but clandestine service that allows white upper-class Puerto Rican men and their sons to maintain their façade of respectability while secretly indulging their sexual fantasies. Her sexual power is not the power to control and humiliate but the power to initiate, teach, and gratify.

Ferré humanizes both Isabels by revealing their antecedents, thoughts, and secret desires. Beneath the sexual advantage of Isabel la Negra and the social advantage of Isabel Luberza, lies the disquieting truth of their unhappiness and unfulfilled desire. Each hankers after what she perceives as the advantage of the other. The black prostitute is the former poor little black girl who yearned to experience the affluence of her social superior, Isabel Luberza. Now transformed into a glorified sex object, she is not satisfied with the role into which she has been forced. Isabel Luberza too is a desiring subject who illustrates the poverty of the affluent white Puerto Rican woman, hankering after the sensual vigor of Isabel la Negra.

The real Isabel Luberza is far less glamorous than the Isabel Luberza imagined by Isabel la Negra. The former appears publicly as the revered decorative appendage but is effectively a figure of the female slave. For slavery, a condition normally associated with the black prostitute's history and her present socioeconomic deprivation, is also a fitting description of the domestic role of her more privileged white counterpart, whose eyes are "enslaved day after day, coming and going, going and coming, measuring the flour and the sugar in the pantry jars, counting again and again the silver cutlery in the dining room coffer to make sure that nothing was missing, calculating the exact amount of food so that there would be no leftovers, so as to be able to go to bed in peace tonight thinking that I have fulfilled my duty, that I have protected your fortune" (41).

In keeping with Ferré's radical feminist orientation, gender assumes primacy over class and race conflict in this story. Equal treatment of both women is a practical illustration of her belief that gender supersedes race and class as a basis for unity among women. Her object is to promote what unites and to subordinate what separates these women. One basis of their unity is their common oppressor: the white man. For it is to the man in their lives, rather than to society or the system, that Ferré ascribes blame for their oppressed and exploited condition and for the enmity between them. Therefore, the option for rebellion and liberation that she advocates is underpinned by gender solidarity. For Ferré, the death of patriarchy is to be achieved by a uniting of poor black and well-to-do white Puerto Rican women against dominant white men. In an act designed to exacerbate the enmity between the two women, Ambrosio wills his estate to his wife and mistress equally. But upon his death, wife and mistress exact revenge on him by frustrating his plans to perpetuate their rivalry. The moment of epiphany comes when each woman sees the other face to face both literally and metaphorically, when their human reality displaces their fictional representation.

The story's well-crafted and intricate structure also illustrates practically the statement the author wishes to make. Ferré uses juxtapositions and simultaneity to shape the theme of the essential identity of Puerto Rican women over and above the circumstantial differences of class and race that may divide them. For Ferré, the high-society lady (dama de sociedad) in Puerto Rico has merely learnt to suppress her sexual desire or is constrained to express it in subtle ways, while the black prostitute is a potential "lady" whose aspirations may have been frustrated. Technical expression of this perceived identity is found on two levels: in overt signs, such as the similarity of their names and their use of the same Cherries Jubilee nail polish, and in the deftly executed and imperceptible shifts from the perspective of one woman to that of the other and the frequent confluence of their narrative voices, so that at times it becomes difficult to distinguish between the two.

Ferré's story has accentuated the specificity of gender relations in Caribbean societies—namely, the way in which problems of race and class inequalities hinder the development of solidarity between women. Yet her vision of the resolution of this conflict falls within the ideal realm of romance.

Rescuing the Slave Woman

Like her male counterpart, the black woman was transplanted to the Caribbean from Africa as slave labor. Caribbean slavery was a complex arrangement. It was born out of economic necessity; the African slave provided the cheap labor on which Europe depended for its capitalist expansion. Although the legal discourse of the period indicates that the colonists in some territories regarded the slaves as humans rather than chattel, the reality was that male and female slaves alike were often brutally exploited. Any discussion of slavery from the perspective of gender must proceed therefore on an understanding of the fact that, in terms of their enslavement, female and male slaves had more to unite than to separate them. With regard to labor function, Gordon K. Lewis notes that the female slave, like her male counterpart, was regarded as "an item of capital equipment . . . dead as to all voluntary agency" (6).

Women worked side by side with men on the plantations, but some division of labor was practiced based on sex and color. Domestic work, though not the preserve of female slaves, was an important area for their employment. The female slave was differentiated from her male counterpart to a certain extent because of her sexual, childbearing, and childrearing functions (Bush, *Slave*, 6). Early scholars represented such work as a promotion in the slave hierarchy, leading to generally more humane treatment. This romantic view appears, for example, in Cuban anthropologist Fernando Ortiz's 1916 account of the "improvement" entailed in the change from field to house slave: "Gone were the dark, smelly slave barracks. The master's leftovers would replace meager rations, . . . there was no more fear of the overseer, and instead sometimes they would receive the kindness of the mistress and the affection of the little white children, reared in the laps of slave women, who were often their wet-nurses" (*Negros,* 284).

In the traditional view, because she benefited from the differential treatment of the sexes, and because of the availability of concubinage as a means of social mobility, the female slave was more submissive and less resisting than her male counterpart. It was also felt that the "domestic" nature of the service required of the child-rearing slave necessarily gave a different quality to her relations with the slave owner. This slave, it was claimed, due to the relatively better treatment received, was bound by feelings of loyalty to her master's family. This is one of the contexts that generated the stereotype of the contented slave.

But this account does not provide a complete picture of the situation of slave women. For example, the sexual exploitation of slave girls by white planters and overseers and the cruel treatment some suffered at the hands of some white wives are well documented. Domestics, slave concubines, and enslaved mothers who bore their white masters' children were not guaranteed preferential treatment. Slave women, in addition, had little or no choice in the matter of the nurturing of their own children, which, for those who worked on the plantations, was subordinated to their labor function. Also well documented are the authorities' deliberate policy of discouraging the formation of permanent slave family units, and the frequent separation of spouses and of children from their parents (Bush, *Slave*, 1–10).

Contemporary Caribbean historians have rejected many of the early versions of slavery. Their research into slavery as experienced by the slaves themselves has resulted in significant new disclosures about the slaves' response to their enslavement. They foreground the variety and nuances in slave responses, especially with respect to covert forms of resistance. In recent times, with the growth of feminist thinking, scholars such as Lucille Mathurin (1975), Rebecca Scott (1985), Hilary Beckles (1988), and Barbara Bush (1990) have rescued the female slave from historical oblivion. Their work has served to contest the prevailing notion of the female slave's passivity and to create a new understanding of her rebellion.

In the Caribbean few slave testimonies have survived the colonial era. To date, the autobiography of the Cuban slave poet Juan Francisco Manzano; *The History of Mary Prince*, narrated by a Jamaican slave woman and edited by Moira Ferguson; and Miguel Barnet's transcription of Esteban Montejo's account of his life as a Cuban slave are unique. Literary representations of slave women have been mainly those produced by white Creole writers in the nineteenth century and those created retroactively in the post-emancipation period. These recent representations have sought to depict the female slave as a human individual, in contrast to the reductive stereotypes of African women popularized since the days of the early European travelers.

One of these retrospectively created literary models of the slave woman portrays her not in her own family nor caring for her own children, but nurturing her master's children. Fernando Ortiz cites legal documents that stipulated how slave children should be cared for:

> Article 8.—Newborn or young black babies whose mothers go to work on the plantations, shall be fed with very light foods, such as soups, gruel, milk etc., until they are weaned and have passed the teething stage.
>
> Article 9.—While their mothers are at work, all the children shall be kept in a house or room to be provided on every sugar or coffee plantation. One female slave or more, as the overseer may deem necessary, or according to the number of children, shall be in charge of them. (*Negros,* 195)

Reality, however, did not always conform to even this prescription, as evidenced in this claim: "Children born to slaves were often neglected abominably, left without hygiene or even much maternal attention after the third day of birth, and infant mortality reached extraordinary numbers. If they survived this experience, slave children began to work at five or six years" (Thomas, 170). Such a lack of concern for the care of slave children is ironically opposed to the frequency with which slave women were required to raise their owners' children.

Because of her place in the slave master's world, writers have portrayed the domestic slave most frequently from the perspective of her relation with and attitude to white authority. The following three poems from Puerto Rico present three different images of the slave woman and three different responses to enslavement. Though the poets are writing about her after the abolition of slavery, they may be seen to participate, albeit unwittingly, in the debate surrounding the institution. One characteristic of ideology is its durability. This point is illustrated by some post-emancipation writers whose perception of the slave woman's behavior implies either a proslavery or an antislavery position.

"My Black Nanny" (La negra que me crió), a poem published by Félix Matos Bernier in 1895, two decades after the abolition of slavery in Puerto

Rico, presents an image of the slave that is the product of a nineteenth-century worldview:

> The black nanny who raised me
> my grandfather never sold her,
> he gave her to me
> like an offering from heaven.
> She was an example for me
> for good and decent was she;
> like a saint she helped my mother
> every moment;
> she died free and honorable,
> and she lives gloriously still
> because I am alive. (qtd. in Morales, 35)

This personal testimony presents us with a view of an individual slave from inside the slave master's world. The poet rejects implicitly the stereotype of the slave as subhuman, which had been used to legitimize the practice of slavery. He has chosen to rehumanize the image of the slave, to celebrate her spiritual and moral attributes, and to immortalize her. His portrayal also contests the antislavery depiction of the relationship between master and slave as that of oppressor and oppressed, found, for example, in some nineteenth-century Caribbean narratives. He offers us instead a picture of the harmonious coexistence of the enslaved and the enslaver.

While the speaker seeks to project a view of the slave woman as docile and submitted to domination, the suspicious reader is likely to be struck by a certain ambiguity in the poem. This poem is, ostensibly, only about the submissive and contented slave. Yet latent in its subtext and competing with the surface level of meaning is a self-legitimating discourse used to create, simultaneously, an image of the master as benevolent. This subliminal message is conveyed quite succinctly in lines 2 to 4, which allude to the commodification of the slave. The reader is meant to infer tacit criticism of the practice from the grandson's apparent endorsement of the grandfather's benevolent action.

However, the ultimate irony of this claim about the "good" slave master is that it contains the naive suggestion that there was a significant difference in the mode of transfer of the slave. With the idea that it is more desirable to make a present of, rather than to sell, a slave, the speaker leaves intact the perception of the slave as chattel. A similar objectification is implicit in the observation about the freedom (and therefore the honor) in which the slave dies. In the view of the speaker, freedom is not a right of this powerless individual, but a concession granted by a humane master. And if one reads the declaration of her immortality in the last two lines in Freudian terms, it indicates that her "dependence" on her master continues even in death. In the final analysis, the image that the poem suppresses (the humane master) is no less significant than the image that it expresses (the submissive slave).

Other hidden and not so commendable assumptions also inhere in this image of meekness. In the first place, the slave woman's value and the poet's admiration for her rest mainly on her usefulness and subservience. Lines 5 and 6 create an impression of her virtue as immanent. This view is promptly erased by lines 7 and 8, which make service the sign of her goodness and decency. In this way the speaker has recorded his approval for the slave's acknowledgment of the superiority of her masters.

Another striking aspect of this poem is the religious vocabulary through which the speaker seeks to elevate the slave. By comparing her to "an offering from heaven," he heightens the process of her reification that was noted earlier. In the same spirit, the characterization of her manner as that of a saint is not a fortuitous one. It suggests an "appropriate" attitude of reverence in the black slave devotee who serves the white goddess. In other words, this image both reflects and legitimizes the stratification of slave society.

One also senses a view of the slave woman, in her docility, as acquiescent to her own enslavement and reconciled to her condition. Her accommodation to slavery is perceived as unproblematic. This is not surprising since the poet draws his impressions from the slave's actions. He does not conceive of the processes that, at the level of her psyche, might have invalidated these impressions.

Orlando Patterson, who has studied extensively the sociology of slavery, offers a different interpretation of this evidence of slave obedience: "While the overt attitudes of the slaves to their masters were clearly those of respect and adoration, one must remain doubtful about the sincerity of their feelings" (173). With specific reference to the stereotype of the submissive slave, Patterson further notes that although it had a "kernel of truth," it might have been the result of socialization or a form of self-fulfilling prophecy: "the subordinate group, in addition to being forced into situations which fulfill the stereotype of the superordinate group, also responds directly to these stereotypes by either appearing to, or actually internalizing them. The slave, in fact, played upon the master's stereotype for his own ends. . . . From the slaves' point of view, this was a direct appeal to, and exploitation of, the inevitable see-what-I-mean mentality of their masters" (179–80). It is precisely this possibility of conflict that Matos Bernier has discounted by patronizing and propagating the idea of the slave woman as docile. He has construed as voluntary compliance what may have been a mechanism for survival or an instance of forced adaptation.

One also finds certain telling areas of silence in the text of the poem. First, consistent with her zombification is the fact that it gives the slave no voice. She is presented from the outside and in vague contours as the Other. Second, despite the intended celebration, she is nameless and therefore depersonalized. Her namelessness belies the claims about her immortality and value, and, in the final analysis, the image comes dangerously close to what Gordon K. Lewis describes as the traditional view of the slave as a "mere cipher, reacting passively to omnipresent oppressive forces" (171). Although the slave nanny has no name, she is identified by her color. This discourse of color perpetuates the European practice of fixing African identity in terms of difference (i.e., nonwhite).

The poem is also conspicuously silent on the question of the slave woman's relation to Africa. By disconnecting her from her African past, the speaker is, willfully or unconsciously, de-emphasizing the deracination suffered by the African through forced transplantation. He sees her as adapted unambiguously to the alien environment of her enslavers. By elevating her to the level of a (Catholic) saint, he expresses the historical importance of the imposed Christian religion as part of the broader deculturation process to which the African was submitted in the New World.

In this depiction of the slave woman, the speaker has deliberately ignored the more disturbing side of her experience, and takes comfort in the illusion that she was contented. In Caribbean slave society such a type would have been similarly celebrated because she would have been perceived to present no threat to the institution of slavery. Here, the poet rejects the dehumanized stereotype of the slave as savage, but simultaneously embraces an equally undesirable one. Some advocates of slavery would have easily endorsed the view of the slave as innocuous and without volition. Though eloquent on the question of the slave's virtue, the speaker is silent on the question of her degraded condition, and is scarcely one remove from the ideology of slave inferiority and the natural supremacy of the ruling class. In this poet's myopically paternalistic view it is easier and more comfortable to celebrate servility, and recognition of the slave woman's humanity is made to appear compatible with acceptance of her enslavement.

An ideological connection may be made between the thinking behind this poem and the standard nineteenth-century rationalization of slavery. The latter took the form of explicit claims of the inferiority of the African and was obviously intended to protect the economic and political status quo. More elusive but equally conservative is the ideology of this writer, who has expressed a favorable attitude toward an individual slave without posing any moral challenge to slavery as an institution. In fact, the ostensible motive of redemption of the slave woman is undercut by what is essentially a defense of the system that oppressed her.

In his 1959 novel *Psyche* Jamaican novelist H. G. DeLisser also chooses to highlight the individual slave's contentment and her enslavers' benevolence: "Yet they liked Psyche; her youth, her looks, her manner, her spirit appealed to them. So for her, on the whole, the voyage had been a very pleasant one" (11). As she leaves the wharf, Psyche comes upon the following scene: "Hogs rooted in the heaps of refuse in the streets, dogs fought one another for the bones they had somehow procured, or wandered idly to and fro. The thoroughfares were full of holes and sandy; there were no sidewalks; the passing of this new batch of slaves scarcely drew anything more than a casual glance or a word or two from the people in the streets." And DeLisser's narrator concludes: "All was sordid, and the sun's heat smote everyone with a pitiless impartiality; *nevertheless, to Psyche it was all wonderful*" (16–17, my emphasis).

This account goes even further than the preceding poem to establish the slave's contentment, through a summary disconnection of the protagonist from her African past:

> She remembered that the evening her village had been attacked she had previously gathered some beans of a plant to dry and crush later on for the doctoring of the spears of those who went out to hunt big game. She had wrapped them up in a piece of pliant kid skin and had snatched up her tiny parcel when about to flee from the hut. She had concealed them in her hair when she knew she was certain to be caught. All the way from Africa she had treasured and hidden them, not because she thought that they were of any value but because they and the anklets and bangles she wore were her only possessions.

Other slaves, she knew, had not even a brass anklet to boast of: nothing except the bush girdle with which they modified their nakedness. But she said nothing about these things now. They seemed utterly unimportant. (20–21)

In a symbolic gesture she marks her detachment from Africa and her adoption of "civilized" habits by changing her anklets for stockings: "She put them away, and this was like saying goodbye to a part of her former life. She knew she would never wear them again" (25).

Other responses of this imaginary slave woman are part of the author's aim to deromanticize Africa. When her master, surprised at her accommodation to her new situation, reminds her that she is a slave, her reply stretches the limits of credibility: "I am freer here than I was in my village ... if I had married that old man I would have been his slave too. I like to be here master—with you" (21). While the historical veracity of the reference to the existence of African slavery is beyond doubt, Psyche's response serves in the present context to minimize the inhumanity of Caribbean slavery. In this account the slave master's benevolence is once again the inevitable counterpart of the slave woman's contentment. Even when the narrator assumes the position of the slave to view the master, from this angle too, the latter's superiority remains unchallenged: "And he was so kind to her ... so superior to every other man that she had ever seen" (22).

The contented slave response is now generally accepted as a surface response. In "Tonga Bambé," Olga Ramírez de Arellano, another Puerto Rican, writing in 1947, contests that one-dimensional view of the passive and mindless workhorse:

> (With her mistress' baby in her arms, Black
> Veve thinks about her native land, about the
> hell of the journey into slavery and about
> her new-found happiness with the white child
> on her lap.)

Black hands, black arms, black face:
"As I rock this linen-white child,
My Katonga heart is born again.
Stars watching over my hut of straw,
My beaming eyes see you again."

"Oh leafy place of shady beauty,
And the sweetness of honey in the coconut trees,

On high, the night of untold anguish
In seesaw motion makes trenches of red;
A boat crossing the spattered waves,
A fire burning with blood and thirst."

Black hands, black arms, black face:
"Now I see my shady arms,
Holding the snowy fruit of the white woman,
Smiling, I open my storehouse of love,
My African milk I give to this child."

Song:
  "Black Veve the white men call me,
In my land I was Tonga Bambé,
And the laughter that floats across the path,
Finds its nest once again in my heart.
Black Veve the white men call me,
In my land I was Tonga Bambé." (qtd. in Morales, 152–53)

This representation of the slave woman bespeaks the post-1940s revision
of the history of the African in the New World, and the displacement of the
superficial and ahistorical *negrista* discourse of the 1920s. In this spirit of
revaluation, contemporary writers have come to view the New World
African, whether slave or free, as both an individual human subject and as
the product of a specific set of historical circumstances.

Although there is some retention of the ideology of the first poem, this
image represents a significant departure from that depiction of the slave
woman. To begin with, the use of a first-person discourse signals a break
with the practice of viewing the slave as the Other. By giving her a voice
and allowing her to use it for self-representation, the poet has added the
interior dimension that is missing from the silhouette image of the slave
in the preceding poem. This poem also departs from earlier tradition in its
focus on the complexity of the slave's posture. The poet has problematized
her response by giving it two dimensions: psychic reality versus surface
appearance.

Tonga Bambé records her experience of dislocation and violation, her
consciousness of, and psychological resistance to, domination, as well as
her adaptation to her situation. She perceives herself as a victim of the
deculturation and psychic mutilation of slavery. Her feeling of exile in the
present is captured brilliantly in her semantic nuances: "Black Veve the
white men call me, / In my land I was Tonga Bambé." In this instance, the

poet avoids the namelessness of the slave in the last poem and makes the very practice of naming a central issue. The name change suffered by the slave is expressive of the process by which Europeans imposed a new identity on the African in the New World, defining him or her in terms of color difference (i.e., the African as black Other and the antithesis of the ideal white Self). This contrasts with the designation of ethnicity (Tonga) in her African name, which therefore becomes the sign for her true identity.

A similar purpose is served by the syntactic distinction between the line "In my land I *was* Tonga Bambé," which expresses the essentiality of her African identity, and the line "Black Veve the white men call me," which implies the persona's psychic distance from an identity that has been foisted upon her. Another change in status implied by the two verbs is the reduction of the former subject ("*I* was") to object ("white men call *me*," my emphasis). There is a similar opposition of the superficial, color-dominated view of the colonizer ("Black hands, black arms, black face") to the protagonist's sense of her essential and authentic being: "My Katonga *heart* is born again" (my emphasis).

Irony is another of the strategies that the persona uses to comment on her present situation. She reproduces the Eurocentric discourse of color, but only to call it into question. Her repeated juxtaposition of her blackness and the whiteness of her masters shows the slave's awareness of the contradictions of a system of hierarchy that privileges white over black. But Tonga Bambé has not internalized the notion of her supposed inferiority or the putative supremacy of her white owners. This is evident in the deliberately heavy-handed emphasis she places on whiteness in the lines "Now I see my shady arms, / Holding the snowy fruit of the white woman." The positioning of "white" to create an inanely repetitive effect after "snowy fruit" tends toward satire. In addition, her reference to her "African milk" that she feeds the white child—that is, the *white* milk of a *black* woman—is a terse way of revealing the absurdity of the prevailing color prejudice. In the final analysis, this image presents to us a slave who, because she has not assimilated the worldview of the dominant group, and because she has psychological confidence in her own self-worth, can distance herself sufficiently to express her repudiation of racist ideology through the use of irony.

However, the poem is not entirely free of ambiguities. In fact, it articulates two discourses that the speaker intends to be complementary, but that in fact compete with each other. The speaker seeks to reconcile the slave's accommodation with her resistance by stressing the restoration of her psychic wholeness after the trauma of displacement. There are two means by which the slave is shown to have achieved this psychic empowerment: through surrogate motherhood and by her abiding memory of Africa.

Acting as the poem's centripetal motif is the visual image of the black slave rocking the white child. First, it suggests that this mother-child interaction provided a harmonious or harmonizing space for the two supposedly antithetical forces in slave society. Second, it is this experience that facilitates the slave's recuperation of her original world: "As I rock this linen-white child / My Katonga heart is born again." And finally it brings psychic healing after the initial trauma of slavery: "And the laughter that floats across the path / Finds its nest once again in my heart."

The attempt to achieve ideological coherence begins with the explanatory note, which, though it precedes the text of the poem and is placed in parentheses, is integral to its ideological interpretation. This note signals the meaning that the poet intends, and it explicitly preempts a reading that would suggest that the slave was unhappy with her lot. Through her preliminary statement, the poet attempts to impose closure on the poem and to ensure the confinement of the reader in the role that Catherine Belsey describes as mere "consumer" of the text (125–29). In effect, the prefatory note is a diversionary strategy that obscures a glaring inconsistency in the poem.

The intended message seems to be that although Tonga Bambé makes a nostalgic return to her lost country and reflects briefly on the trauma of the Middle Passage, she has also transcended both the loss and the trauma to find happiness and meaning in her present circumstances. As in the first poem, where the slave's value is tied to service, the happiness of this slave derives from the satisfaction of nurturing the master's child. Africa represents her lost paradise, but through mothering she has found a new heaven. With the creation of this image, the poem appears to be a celebration of motherhood and, more specifically, the triumph of maternal love over any resentment for the violence of slavery. Such an emphasis on the slave's role of mother effectively displaces antislavery sentiment from the poem's center. By subordinating the social death of the transplanted African woman to her psychic rebirth, the poem leaves intact the image of the contented slave articulated by the supporters of the institution of slavery.

It is true that the relations between master and slave were not uniform, and that while there were various forms of resistance on the part of the slaves, they were also forced eventually, in most cases, to adapt to their new

condition. Gordon Lewis, among others, has recognized the survival motive in the posture of accommodation, under which the slaves often dis-
guised different forms of subversion (175–76). It is within this context of
resistance that the poet seeks to place Tonga Bambé's adaptation to slavery.
While this poem, unlike the first, does not evade the conflict underlying
the slave's situation, its too facile resolution of this conflict foregrounds its
own ideological wavering.

The final image of the contented slave seems to be at odds with both her
awareness of her situation of exile and the psychological resistance she
offers in the face of a system that seeks to degrade her. There is also the
suggestion that the opportunity to mother her master's child is a boon of
slavery, a form of compensation sufficient to erase the violence she has
suffered. Not only does this vision seem analogous to the argument about
the slave's natural docility, but by admitting positive possibilities in slavery, the poet stops short of the unequivocal criticism demanded by the
degradation of the slave woman in this social order.

The poet is careful, however, not to interpret the slave's accommodation
as a sign of the isolation from Africa seen in the last poem. Tonga Bambé
uses a first-person discourse not only for self-definition but also to evoke
and reconnect with Africa. Her memory helps her to transcend the distance between her African home and the alien land. But the idea of Africa
projected by the poem is the construct of a Western consciousness and
more akin to a Romantic paradise: "Oh leafy place of shady beauty, / And
the sweetness of honey in the coconut trees." Thus, despite the attempt to
present a positive image of Africa, the Afrocentric potential of the poem is
not fully realized.

Nineteenth-century Cuban narrative has furnished a clear illustration
of the mediating role of politics in the cultural domain. In the first place,
slaves were denied access to education and the other means of literary
production. Secondly, in the early part of the century, general censorship
of the expression of antislavery sentiment prevented the publication of all
but specially commissioned novels on the subject of slavery. In fact, some
novels written during the period did not appear in print before the twentieth century. These novels, commonly referred to as antislavery, were
intimately bound up with the reformist agenda of a sector of Cuba's ruling
class, whose intent was to bring about better treatment of slaves but not to
promote abolition. Domingo del Monte, a liberal white Cuban, was the
main figure associated with this reformist crusade, which he organized
through a literary circle of white Creole intelligentsia, some of them slave

owners. Therefore, the twin constraints of self-interest and censorship circumscribed nineteenth-century novelists' portrayal of the slaves.

Female slaves feature in the most well known of these works. They are the protagonists in Félix Tanco y Bosmoniel's *Petrona y Rosalía* (1838) and Francisco Calcagno's *Los crímenes de Concha* (1881). In other novels such as Antonio Zambrana's *El negro Francisco* (1873), Anselmo Suárez y Romero's *Francisco* (1880), and Villaverde's *Cecilia Valdés* they are significant figures. White Creole Cuban writers generally depicted their female slave characters as Romantic stereotypes. Following the mandate to present a moderate view of the slaves' response to bondage, some of these novelists portrayed slave women primarily as victims. The victimhood of the mulatto slave was also substantially different from the victimhood of the black slave. For example, the mulatto Camila's tragedy in *El negro Francisco* comes not from physical ill-treatment by her masters but from her frustrated love for the black slave Francisco. Dorotea, her counterpart in *Francisco,* suffers a similar fate.

If the *mulata* is a figure of incredible beauty in these novels, the black woman is a figure of incredible strength, withstanding brutal work and punishment on the sugar estates. Although Concha, the protagonist of Francisco Calcagno's *Los crímenes de Concha,* is a hapless victim whose misery is relieved only by her death, neither hard work nor brutal punishment crushes the black slave Petrona in Felix Tanco y Bosmoniel's *Petrona y Rosalía.* In these reformist accounts of the slave woman's experience of bondage, the emphasis is on physical abuse and sexual exploitation, on victimhood without hope. Her incredible strength helps her to survive, but her response is essentially passive.

These novels, though intended to show sympathy for the slaves and their plight, cannot be said to be opposed to slavery. Seen through essentially proslavery eyes, the posture of helpless compliance is scarcely distinguishable from that of willing subservience. The slave woman in the first instance is wretched but denied the desire or capacity for rebellion. In the other, by reason of her contentment, she feels no real need to rebel.

But not all the fictional slave women conform to this victim stereotype. Some stand out as figures of resistance. Cirilio Villaverde is somewhat less restrained in focusing on slave discontent in *Cecilia Valdés* (1839, 1882). He allows María de Regla in the same novel to voice the slave woman's suffering. Villaverde devotes several pages of the novel to this character, allowing her to give her subjective account of her experience and to protest against the injustice of her bondage. She speaks bitterly of the cruelty of being forced to nurse her mistress's child while neglecting her own, and she bemoans the injustice of the deliberate destruction of her family.

However, her posture is not without ambivalence, reflecting, perhaps, Villaverde's ambivalence and that of his class toward the institution of slavery. In the first place, María de Regla, like Juan Francisco Manzano in his *Autobiografía* (1840), is careful to link her earlier contentment to the benevolence of her previous masters and to affirm her conformity to her slave status. Of her husband and children she says: "I do not complain because they serve the masters, they are slaves and have to serve. . . . I complain because we are separated (II:220). Moreover, she trivializes her dream of freedom: "Each time I hear it I lose my mind, I dream of it day and night, I build castles, I see myself in Havana surrounded by my husband and children, going to dances dressed in frills, with gold mantillas, coral earrings, satin shoes, and silk stockings" (II:227). In contrast, the novel is more summary in its treatment of its most recalcitrant black female slave, the strong and proud Tomasa, a runaway who refuses to submit to punishment and maintains a stoically defiant posture in the face of the most brutal flogging.

Writers in the foregoing illustrations claimed for themselves the authority to speak for the slaves. In a poem from the postcolonial period, however, the voice of the slave woman is the voice of categorical resistance. Criticism of slavery is the primary objective of "Black Kandala's Story" (Historia de Kandala la Negra), published by Puerto Rican poet Lauro Martínez between 1941 and 1965. Like "Tonga Bambé" this poem is an imaginary slave woman's account of her New World experience:

"Because I am black the people say
That I have no heart.
Oh, dear God, how they treat us!
Humiliation is our lot."

"They don't know," said the Congo slave,
"That I, a young girl, a young man once loved.
That African brave and strong,
His love as tender as a babe's.

I still remember that tragic night
The slave trader came
He killed my mother, he killed my father,
And me he put right into chains.

With me were other captives,
There too was my faithful Barick:
My faithful lover, my brave Congo man,
Whom I loved with passion wild.

A sight to see: his Herculean body
stood out above that crowd;
Barick, my lover, How lovely you looked!
Proud and stately like a lion.
How hard you fought
The attack of that traitor,
That wretched slave trader, his heart like a devil,
The assassin of our love

. . . .
Where did they take him, where did they sell him
My black Congo man, my faithful lover?
Oh, if he only knew that I still love him,
And that my love is his alone!" (qtd. in Zenón Cruz, 146–47)

The problem in this account is with the voice that speaks, not with the sentiments it expresses. Like the author of "Tonga Bambé," this poet recognizes that once the slave woman is given a voice, she will naturally use it to express some form of protest. But whereas Tonga Bambé uses her voice to make ironic commentary on her situation, a more recalcitrant Kandala expresses her psychological resistance with vehemence.

This African slave is implacable in her condemnation of the physical and psychological violence of transplantation, and unequivocal in her denunciation of slavery. She creates a Manichean split between slave and enslaver, and reflected in the stridency of the language in which she condemns the enslaver is an attitude of continuing resentment and resistance. She admits no compensation for the loss of previous happiness. In her representation of the slave experience as personal annihilation, and in her final insistence on the continuation of her emotional trauma due to the loss of her African lover, Kandala therefore subverts the notion of contentment or adaptation to bondage, seen in the previous poems.

Kandala cites her love experience for the explicit purpose of undermining the ideology of the slave as subhuman. By focusing on this experience, the poet endows the slave woman with human feelings, countering in this way the myth created to naturalize her subjugation under slavery. The slave's account of the trauma suffered because of the cruel separation from her lover serves as the basis for her strong protest against her enslavement. This protest interlocks with an Afrocentric discourse as a corrective to the Eurocentric depreciation of Africa and Africans.

Memory helps Kandala to recuperate her African past, but her story does not have the happy resolution of "Tonga Bambé." Her evocation of Africa merely underlines her tragedy. Kandala's profession of her continuing love for her African lover translates into a will to resist psychic annihilation and to remain unrelentingly attached to her homeland. The paradigm of civilized (Europe) and savage (Africa) is inverted in the respective images of the enslaver ("devil," "assassin") and her Congo lover ("faithful," "brave," "proud," "strong," "dignified"). And again, as in "Tonga Bambé," national identity displaces the discourse of color through the use of the epithets "African" and "Congo" to refer to her lover.

However, despite this desire to endow the slave with an Afrocentric vision, as with the last poem, the strategy used is counterproductive for the effect sought. Mediating the speaker's subjectivity is the Eurocentric consciousness that controls her voice. She portrays her lover through the use of vocabulary with distinctly Romantic overtones. In particular, the image of his Herculean body is reminiscent of Barbara Bush's observation about the ludicrous and demeaning classical names, such as Hercules and Phibia, that were given to the slaves and that stripped them of their African identity (*Slave*, 52). With his apparently limited knowledge of Africa and his inability to perceive the African in African terms, Martínez can only project this "enlightened" image by resorting to the anachronistic discourse of Romantic idealization.

As in the previous poem, the decolonizing impetus that drives contemporary historians is evident in the use of the image of the slave to displace the negative stereotype of the African woman's animal sensuality. Like Ramírez de Arellano, Martínez creates the illusion that he is presenting the slave woman from her own viewpoint. He also generates, obliquely, an idea of Africa in the process. But this project, commendable though it may be, is undercut somewhat by the intractability of the influence of the inherited European discourse.

Historical and literary discourses converge in the revisionist perspective of slave resistance in "Tonga Bambé" and "Black Kandala's Story." The images are also important conveyers of ideology, and when dismantled they betray contradictions where the poets intend ideological cohesion. In the final analysis, the insidious presence of the very ideology that the poets set out to subvert aborts or diminishes their potentially rehabilitative projects.

Tragic Mammies and Passive Workhorses

Since the socio-racial structure inherited from the colonial period has maintained much of its original configuration, and blacks are the main constituents of the laboring class, it is not surprising that the black woman also appears in a nurturing role in the post-emancipation period. A recurrent mode for the depiction of this type in Spanish Caribbean literature is the personal testimony of a white persona who has had a close relationship with a black nanny or servant. These testimonies usually present her as a moral guide or as a positive affective influence, pointing up one of the ironies of race relations in the Caribbean, where the social inferiority of this woman is not seen to be incompatible with these roles. Celebration tinged with nostalgia defines such portrayals.

Another Puerto Rican poet, Vicente Palés Matos, whose published works date from 1945, composed a poem that also bears the title "My Black Nanny" (La negra que me crió). The repetition of the title of the earlier poem invites a comparison of the two discourses and their corresponding ideologies. This speaker also pays tribute to the black nursemaid of his childhood:

All my life I will remember
the black nanny who raised me:
her sweet compassionate eyes
bending over the stove,
the fat bosom she gave me,
her calico apron.

She laughed a laugh like honey
showing her teeth white like rice.
In her lap my childhood found the refuge
of a nest of cotton.

There in the village
(some goats, a burning sun)
she was the welcome black shade:
protecting trunk of the silk-cotton tree

. . . .

At night sleep overcame me
as I listened to the magic of her voice,
or as her tales of ghosts and phantoms
stirred me with terror within.

She passed from this life to the next.
I don't remember how she went.
They found her huddled
like a dog in a corner.

I cried all day
for my black nanny,
fearing always that she would say,
hearing me weeping in the parlor,
with her soothing mother's voice,
"My little one, please . . . !" (qtd. in Morales, 105–6)

Palés Matos, like Matos Bernier, uses the autobiographical voice as a strategy for authenticating his representation. However, the perception of the nanny shifts noticeably in the second poem. This may be attributed to the change in the legal status of the black woman and to the availability of alternative images propagated mainly by nationalist ideology.

One can read the second poem as a reaction against the dehumanized stereotype of the slave in the first on several counts. Although both speakers acknowledge the immortality of the servant's spirit, the self-centeredness of the declaration "and she lives gloriously still / because I am alive" in the first is replaced in the second by a more intense focus on the attributes that have contributed to that immortality. Emotive epithets predominate in the language of the second poem, suggesting a more authentic human relationship based on love. The speaker deliberately invests the servant's physical traits with affective rather than racial or aesthetic value ("her sweet compassionate eyes," "she was the welcome black shade," "the magic of her voice"). Obviously, this poem draws on an existing stereotype of womanhood: that of the idealized mother who is self-denying in her generosity, protecting and undemanding, who lives to serve, who expects and gets nothing in return. More specifically, this figure is a version of the stereotype of the black mammy who, according to Barbara Christian, also appears in southern white American literature as fat, nurturing, kind, and above all strong and enduring (2).

In the reference to the nursemaid's death are intimations of the material conditions of her existence. Strong implications of social disadvantage underlie this account of the end of one who gave selflessly but died like a dog. Irony is apparent in the very structural imbalance of the poem, where the elaborate details of the six stanzas describing her role as nurturer underline the pathos of the single stanza that records, cursorily and without comment, the circumstances of her death. Yet even this is an implicitly self-indicting strategy, as the egocentric sentimentality of the speaker's nostalgia takes precedence over critical confrontation of the woman's social plight. While he affirms her goodness and acknowledges her exemplary influence, he shows little concern for her outside this role. His insensitivity is made even more poignant by the offhand treatment of her horrible death, a treatment that is reinforced by the abruptness of the end-stopped lines: "She passed from this life to the next. / I don't remember how she went." This poem gives yet another indication of how the working-class black woman has been valued in her stereotypical role of servant and mother-surrogate, but not in the full extent of her individuality and humanity.

Pura del Prado, an expatriate Cuban poet, has also created a version of this image of the black woman in a poem entitled "Granny" (Abuele):

> Leonor, the sweet black washerwoman,
> pure woman of simple solitude,
> she taught me how to spell from a book
> and how to breathe deep in the spring time.
>
> On the ground in her patio near the almond trees,
> I kept fireflies and a honeycomb,
> and in her wee little wooden house
> I learnt to kiss on the cheek.
>
> Leonor wore golden earrings,
> in a trunk she kept, like a treasure,
> postcards which her kindness gave me.
>
> Because of her my heart is mulatto
> I love the pain of kinky hair
> and the sadness of dark skin. (qtd. in Ruiz del Vizo, Poesía, 106–7)

For her tribute this poet has chosen the classical form of the sonnet. She too records a feeling of nostalgia for the washerwoman, and celebrates the love and tenderness that characterized their relationship. Like the nursemaid in the last poem, the washerwoman supplants the biological mother in the affective development of the child. Both poems juxtapose the black woman's material impoverishment with the wealth of her positive spiritual and emotional attributes.

A clear difference in this last poem, however, is anticipated in the title, with its connotations of the closeness of a blood relationship. By avoiding the generic namelessness of the two earlier figures, del Prado has ascribed a greater degree of individuality to the black servant. Perhaps the most significant aspect of del Prado's depiction, however, is that it illuminates that area of the washerwoman's existence that the other two poems obscure—namely, the suffering that derives from racial prejudice. The speaker has therefore not idealized the black woman out of her real social context.

These poems represent a gradation in the treatment of the black woman in her role as servant-nurturer: from the matter-of-factness of the first bald statement ("She was an example for me / for good and decent was she"), to the more humanized and emotional portraiture of the second, and then to the human and social sensitivity of the vision of Pura del Prado. Yet even this last poet's recognition of the woman's suffering is expressed as a feeble lament, and the tone of even this nostalgic evocation is sentimental rather than critical.

Black surrogate mothers occupy central positions in the impoverished white Creole families of the postcolonial fictional worlds created by Dominican novelists Jean Rhys and Phyllis Allfrey. Reminiscent of the slave in Felix Matos Bernier's poem ("My Black Nanny"), Christophine, the black obeahwoman from Martinique in Rhys's *Wide Sargasso Sea* (1966), was a wedding present to Antoinette's mother. Christophine not only provides a partial antidote to young Antoinette's alienation but later becomes the one to whom Antoinette turns for counsel:

"Christophine, he does not love me, I think he hates me. . . . What shall I do? . . ."
"You ask me a hard thing, I tell you a hard thing, pack up and go."
. . .
"But there must be something else I can do."

She looked gloomy. "When man don't love you, more you try, more he hate you, man like that. If you love them they treat you bad, if you don't love them they after you night and day bothering your soul case out. . . ."
"When must I go, where must I go?"
"But look me trouble, a rich white girl like you and more foolish than

the rest. A man don't treat you good, pick up you skirt and walk out."
(109)

Lally, the old black nurse in Allfrey's *The Orchid House* (1954), is a perpetuation of the black mammy stereotype, and is driven by unswerving loyalty and deep devotion to her white Creole family:

> she went into another room and came back with a basket in her arms, and in the basket was a little baby—that was Miss Stella. I looked into the basket: ... and there lying on a little cushion was the prettiest girl-child I had ever seen. Then this young lady lifted her baby out of the basket in a very awkward way, so that I couldn't help taking the baby from her and showing her how to do it properly. From that moment I loved Madam and I loved Miss Stella and I knew that I would not leave them until they did not need me any longer. (10)

Allfrey has chosen her to be the consciousness and insight behind the narrative that recounts the family's decay. In their novels these two writers have repositioned the black surrogate mothers (the viewed subjects of the Hispanic examples), making them privileged viewers and giving them new roles as prisms that refract white Creole images. The sense of tragedy in the lives of their Hispanic equivalents finds no echo in these characters.

Consciousness of the material condition of the poor in the Caribbean's social arrangements was evident only sporadically before the twentieth century, and the development of a literary protest tradition had been retarded largely by the burden of the colonial heritage. However, the political and ideological developments associated with the Second World War had their repercussions on Caribbean cultural life. Exposure to revolutionary ideologies caused many Caribbean writers to look at their societies and to depict them in ways that would disturb rather than lead to complacency.

Cuba stands out among the Spanish Caribbean islands, and even in the rest of the Caribbean, because of the early appearance of sustained protest in its nineteenth-century narratives. Despite its failings and contradictions, Cuban antislavery literature is an important precursor for later Cuban writers. This, in fact, explains why as early as 1930, when many Caribbean writers were still refusing to confront their social realities, and *negrista* distortions of the Negro were dominant, some Cuban writers had already begun to introduce social criticism into their representations of the Afro-Caribbean experience. In the early stages of the *negrista* movement, the obsession with the Afro-Caribbean woman as an erotic creature had the effect of obscuring her social situation. Guillén's *Motivos de son* (1930), as we have seen, was one of the earliest attempts to divert attention from her sensuality and highlight her lived reality.

In its political dimension, the institution of slavery had enabled the domination of the laboring class by the planter class. An obvious vestige of this past is the persistent blackness of poverty in the Caribbean. Five hundred years after their transplantation to the New World as slaves, manual labor is still the primary function of black people. The working-class woman is typically black and performs laboring and service functions that are the contemporary equivalents of her slave roles.

In 1930, the same year that Guillén's *Motivos de son* appeared, another Cuban poet, Emilio Ballagas, published a poem in which he lamented the death of the famous Afro-Cuban dancer María Belén Chacón:

> In the rumba skies
> no longer will shine
> your constellation of curves
> . . . .
> María Belén Chacón, María Belén Chacón . . .
> What bark bit your lung?
> It was no bark, no nail
> No nail, no spell
> It was that iron, in the early morning, that ruined your lung!
>   (qtd. in Morales, 384)

The poet uses the elegiac mode to mourn the dancer's death and, by foregrounding its cause, to make an implicit statement against her social plight. Through the ironic juxtaposition of her entertainment value and the economic deprivation that indirectly caused her death, he deliberately undercuts the apparent celebration of the dancer's erotic qualities.

In her address to the black dancer, Cuban poet Carmen Cordero goes beyond the implicit critique of Ballagas and seeks to propel the *rumbera* from passivity to political action:

> Black rumba dancer, dance no more
> the black dance of the banana walks.
> Your people are suffering, suffering
> under the tyrants' absurd laws.
>
> Black rumba dancer, while you give
> wanton pleasure to the crazy eyes

of the white man, you blind your eyes
to the bloody struggles of your brothers.

Black rumba dancer, stop that dance.
You see the bellies of the wicked master
filled to excess . . . and you without your ration . . .

Down with the rhythms, take up your sword.
Open the furrows of hope
on the path of your perdition. (qtd. in Morales, 428–29)

With this militant attitude the speaker abandons the objectivist *negrista* posture and uses the more rhetorically powerful form of direct address and exhortation. This poem gives primacy to racial and social dichotomy and black poverty and oppression, echoing Ballagas's protest against the exploitation of the *rumbera* for entertainment by the white ruling class. By emphasizing her social disadvantage, the speaker refuses the nonthreatening image preferred by the majority of *negrista* poets and advocates an alternative role for the *rumbera* as an agent of social change.

Of the three Spanish territories, the Dominican Republic offers the smallest body of literature about the woman of African extraction. However, Manuel del Cabral stands out in the first half of the twentieth century as one of the few writers from that country to demonstrate more than a perfunctory interest in the black experience. His most important published work on this theme, *Trópico negro,* appeared in 1941. By this time the new imperative of social criticism had begun to replace the *negrista* emphasis on sensationalism and *costumbrista* documentation of Afro-Caribbean folklore. In the 1930s, Cuban poet Nicolás Guillén, with his *Motivos de son* (1930), *Sóngoro cosongo* (1931), and *West Indies Ltd.* (1934), had provided the ideological leadership for the protest movement.

Cabral wrote his *Trópico negro* in this vein of social protest. He does not view the experience of blacks as separable from their experience of being exploited. Poems like "Pulula" expose their plight in a capitalist economic order:

Black Pulula, how well
you iron the clothes of others.
When will you iron your face;
that map of pain!

Pulula, little Pulula,
you are the load and you are the mule.

With your little magic amulet
it is no secret that it is stone;
it is alive and it is a stiff,
it will not look you in the eye,
it will not look at you,
it still looks
to the other side.

But, Pulula,
why do you wait,
why not cure your deaf Saint Benito?

. . . .

With an amulet so white
your luck is so black,
maybe a black charm
will bring you white luck

. . . .

Tell your pinewood saint
tell him to spend a whole day
in your hut filled with holes:
for in every saint made of wood
there may be a carpenter.

Pulula, little Pulula,
you are the load and you are the mule.
Forget your shame and ask
your magic statue
not to sleep in your house.
Let him come with tools;
a hammer, nails and wood;
let him come to mend your cot;
do not have him mend your soul! (qtd. in Morales, 229–31)

This poem is an example of the underlying contradictions in certain attempts at vindication of the Negro. On the one hand, Pulula stands as an
emblem of the working-class black woman, exploited and economically
deprived. The image of bestial docility used to characterize her is reminiscent of the perception of the speaker in "The Black Woman Grinds Her
Grain" (La negra muele su grano), written at approximately the same time
by Puerto Rican poet Evaristo Ribera Chevremont. In that poem, the toil-

ing woman is depicted with stereotypical racist overtones as a "docile beast."

But while the discourse in that instance reinforces the stereotype through overt means and affirms this attitude as essential, "Pulula" seemingly suggests that docility is an externally imposed condition. The poet has used ironing—her typical labor activity—to make an ironic statement about the fact that this woman gives her service to make easier the life of her social superiors, while she is unable to relieve her own suffering. In this respect, del Cabral's protest has progressed beyond Vicente Palés Matos's intimations of the woman's social disadvantage. He confronts directly the anomaly in the working-class woman's social situation.

Despite the poem's focus on the laundress's pitiful situation, the incisive irony and sarcasm to which the speaker has recourse in his representation of the role of religion and superstition in her life are counterproductive. It appears that his purpose is to prod the woman into an awareness of the conservative function of religion and superstition. It may even be his way of instigating a repudiation of this fruitless ideology in favor of a more productive social activism. But by focusing mainly on her practice of religion and its retarding effect on her socioeconomic status, he preempts the promised denunciation of the system of power relations that has created her plight. The targets of the poem's mockery and sarcasm are not only the religious practices and symbols, but also the woman who puts her faith in them. As a result we are left with an image of this working-class woman as being less a victim of an oppressive system, and more the agent of her own oppression: "When will *you* iron your face / that map of pain!" (my emphasis). Because she embraces religious beliefs that are materially useless and irrelevant to her social needs, the poet would have her bear the primary responsibility for her condition and the brunt of the speaker's criticism.

Besides this, the poem ends with a fatalistic conclusion about the working-class black woman's destiny:

Pulula, but Pulula,
today at six,
who will come to iron your face?
Who?
There is but one ironing woman
who, like you, irons so well.
How starched and how hard
will your face be then!

> With a white iron of stone
> from head down to the toes,
> death,—your ironing woman—
> see how she has ironed your skin! (qtd. in Morales, 231)

In these final stanzas, the denial of the woman's potential for changing her condition conflicts with the poet's earlier perception of her as an active participant in a historical process. For this poet, the victimization of the black woman is a social tragedy—reprehensible but also irreversible. His denunciation is the lament of one who does not conceive of the possibility of her social liberation; she can achieve personal liberation only through death.

Del Cabral's protest against the woman's condition is therefore attenuated both by the choice of discursive strategy and the myopia and confusion of his social vision. Because of the implacability of his ironic tone, the poet has created a very unsympathetic picture of this individual. In the end, she appears tragically pathetic, for the poet's social awareness still does not lead him to challenge the notion of the natural docility of the Negro. By claiming that this woman is responsible for her state, the poet offers a perspective that those who seek to naturalize the existing social order could easily appropriate.

Social critique is also the objective of "Black Woman from Trinidad" (Negra de Trinidad), published in 1963 by Puerto Rican poet Vicente Geigel Polanco:

> I saw the procession of market women
> moving through the lanes of Trinidad.
> Gloomily, slowly they moved, driven
> by the early morning routine.

> Trays on their heads,
> making their way to the daily struggle for bread,
> from five to six in the morning
> I watched them file through the city.

> . . . .

> Ignoring each other, immutable
> not muttering a word,
> living all together
> the same tragic fate.

> Gloomily, slowly, they moved, driven
> by the morning routine.

> Black their skin, black their destiny
> . . . .
>
> Black woman turned shadow, sexless black woman,
> black woman without soul, without will,
> without hope of a better life
> in the green isle of Trinidad. (qtd. in Morales, 114–15)

Although this perspective suggests criticism of the system that oppresses the woman of this class, it also coincides with Del Cabral's fatalistic perception of her destiny. This poet's view of the system as given leads to a denial of the black woman's will or ability to change her condition. He echoes the very deterministic arguments on which the original rationalization of black oppression under slavery was predicated.

These representations contrast with the more optimistic outlook that informs the writings of Caribbean poets from other territories. In "Market Women," Jamaican poet Daisy Myrie depicts her female peasants not as victims but as economic agents:

> Down from the hills, they come
> With swinging hips and steady stride
> To feed the hungry Town.
> They stirred the steep dark land
> To place within the growing seed.
> And in the rain and sunshine
> Tended the young green plants,
> They bred, and dug and reaped.
> And now, as Heaven has blessed their toil,
> They come, bearing the fruits,
> These hand-maids of the Soil,
> Who bring full baskets down,
> To feed the hungry Town. (qtd. in Figueroa, 10)

A similarly romantic image is created by Jamaican poet George Campbell in "Market Women" (1945), but one also glimpses an awareness of their contribution to economic life: "These people with their golden fruit / Their black hands offer golden suns" (40).

The following example from Haitian poetry presents the black peasant women as possessing the potential for self-liberation and the power of social transformation. Carl Brouard metaphorizes their emblem, the broom, to underline their potential for political action:

You, you peasant women who come down from our hills
With brat in your belly
You whores dragging your fly-laden stinks
All of you, the mob,
Rise up
And swipe the broom wide. (qtd. in Hoffmann, 97)

George Campbell also forges an image of working-class black women as agents of change. He writes in "History makers" (1945):

Women stone breakers
Hammers and rocks
Tired child makers
Haphazard frocks
Strong thigh . . .
Hard white piles
Of stone
Under hot sky
In the gully bed
No smiles
No sigh
No moan . . .
Destiny shapers
History makers
Hammers and rocks. (qtd. in Figueroa, 66)

Eschewing lament, Campbell celebrates, very economically, the black women's strength, without obscuring the protest against their socioeconomic condition. As a residue of slavery, manual labor and the black people who perform it have been ascribed the lowest value in Caribbean society. Here, the poet sets out to remove the traditional stigma associated with this form of work. He invests their hammers with metaphorical value in order to endow the black women who wield them with the creative capacity to effect change in the very system that oppresses them. From apparent victims engaged in alienated and alienating mechanical labor in the first stanza ("No smiles / No sigh / No moan"), they are transformed into a political force in the second, with the capacity, it is implied, to become the willful shapers and makers of a better future.

These poets, then, seem to be united in their bid to create consciousness of the social condition of this group of Afro-Caribbean women. Social consciousness, however, also requires an appropriate response in the poet. The protest against the social plight of the working-class woman is sometimes quite ambiguous, and even counterproductive. Sometimes the images created for this purpose betray the insidious presence of ideologies that undermine the intended vindication. While the Hispanophone poets seem to embrace the cause of the black underclass, the pessimism that colors their vision serves, in effect, merely to reiterate the age-old notion of the inferior status of black people as predestined.

The Black Woman and the Cuban Revolution

Predictably enough, the political transformation brought about by the 1959 Revolution, its ideological premises, and its particular brand of cultural politics have made their impact on literary practice in Cuba. One manifestation of this has been the consistent efforts by many postrevolution writers to transform earlier discourses used to treat the black experience. By the advent of the Revolution, *costumbrista* interest in the Negro was already on the decline in Cuba, and poets, such as Nicolás Guillén, had changed the ideological direction of their work and adopted the view of the social experience of Afro-Caribbean people as part of an international system of domination and exploitation of the masses. Contemporary Cuban poets have tended to define the Negro in national rather than racial terms. For many postrevolution poets, the problem of race has ceased to be an issue separable from the class struggle.

In 1975 Nancy Morejón, the most well known female Afro-Cuban poet, published "Black Woman" (Mujer negra). It is an outstanding depiction of the Afro-Caribbean woman seen through the lens of revolutionary ideology:

> I still smell the foam of the sea they made me cross.
> The night, I can't remember it.
> The ocean itself could not remember that.
> But I can't forget the first gull I made out in the distance.
> High, the clouds, like innocent eye-witnesses.
> Perhaps I haven't forgotten my lost coast,
> nor my ancestral language.
> They left me here and here I've lived.
> And because I worked like an animal,
> here I came to be born.
> How many Mandinga epics did I look to for strength

I rebelled.

His worship bought me in a public square.
I embroidered His Worship's coat and bore him a male child.
My son had no name.
And His Worship died at the hands of an impeccable English lord.

I walked.

This is the land where I suffered
mouth-in-the-dust and the lash.
I rode the length of all its rivers.
Under its sun I planted seeds, brought in the crops,
but never ate those harvests.
A slave barracks was my house,
built with stones that I hauled myself.
While I sang to the pure beat of native birds.

I rose up.

In this same land I touched the fresh blood
and decayed bones of many others,
brought to this land or not, the same as I.
I no longer dreamt of the road to Guinea.
Was it to Guinea? Benin? To Madagascar? Or Cape Verde?

I worked on and on.

I strengthened the foundations of my millenary song and of my
hope.

I left for the hills.

My real independence was the free slave fort
and I rode with the troops of Maceo.
Only a century later,
together with my descendants,
from a blue mountain.

I came down from the Sierra

to put an end to capital and usurer,
to generals and to bourgeois.
Now I exist: only today do we own, do we create.
Nothing is foreign to us.

The land is ours.
Ours the sea and the sky,
the magic and the vision.
Compañeros, here I see you dance
around the tree we are planting for communism.
Its prodigal wood resounds. (Weaver, 87–89)

The ideological parameters within which this vision of the Afro-Cuban woman unfolds are clearly shaped by the poet's own historical vantage point. Her vision is diachronic: the reconstruction of the Afro-Cuban woman's historical and psychological journey spans the transplantation from Africa and plantation slavery, the independence struggles and nationalist movement, and the Castro Revolution and its aftermath. History functions as both a structuring device and a theme in the poem, which locates the black woman in the context of Cuban history and is also a conscious meditation on that history.

Morejón's account of the black woman's journey from Africa to the Caribbean and of the process of transformation of her African identity into that of the Creole gives a new slant to the revisionist perspective, previously noted as the dominant motive of recent Caribbean historiography. Beginning with the Middle Passage journey, the speaker de-emphasizes the often-cited trauma of the diasporic experience. She records her responses by using a markedly nonemotive discourse, thus separating the poem from the tradition of sentimental antislavery literature. There is no expression of self-pity or any lament that might evoke pathos or reinforce the notion of slave passivity. Morejón's persona foregrounds not the victimhood and martyrdom of her enslavement, but her strength and indestructible capacity for survival.

Subtlety, indirection, and ellipsis are the means employed to convey protest against her slave experience. The line "I embroidered His Worship's coat and bore him a male child" is more powerful in its impact because the disconnection between embroidering for her master and bearing his child points starkly to the reality of the sexual exploitation of the black woman that is immanent in the history of slavery. Similarly, the discrepancy between her instrumentality in supporting the economic system and her economic deprivation is encapsulated in the ironic twist given by "[I] never ate" to the preceding "I planted" and "[I] brought in the crops." These lines also allude to the Marxist view of slavery as one instance of alienated, noncreative labor. Through such expressions of protest, Morejón, in an implicit but unequivocal manner, repudiates pro-slavery ideology and, more specifically, the stereotype of the contented slave.

In charting the Afro-Cuban woman's historical course beyond the experience of slavery, this poem also speaks to the question of her psychological relationship to her African origins. Edward Brathwaite has used the term the African "heartland" to indicate the spiritual connection of the New World slaves to their cultural roots ("African," 81), and Gordon K. Lewis treats the slave subculture, with its "emphatic *africanía*," as a form of protest and assertion (185–86). In the case of the slave persona Tonga Bambé, as we saw earlier, her ability to remember her real name and her evocation of home were indices of both temporal and spiritual proximity to Africa.

The contemporary descendant of the slave woman in Morejón's poem recognizes this African continuity, but with apparent reluctance and without lament: "Perhaps I haven't forgotten my lost coast, / nor my ancestral language." Here the use of the nonaffirmative ("perhaps") has the effect of diminishing the notion of continuity—a curious stance when one considers the bold affirmations of the African connection found in the work of Morejón's compatriot, Nicolás Guillén, and in French *négritude* poetry, and established by many anthropological studies of the Caribbean. It is a statement that also appears to minimize the inescapable reality of African retentions in language, and the African-European syncretism now accepted as the constitutive element of many aspects of Cuban culture.

An even stronger expression of dissociation from the African past is contained in the lines "How many Mandinga epics did I look to for strength / I rebelled." The persona moderates the standard interpretation of slavery as a process of involuntary cultural mutilation and represents it as a conscious act of disconnection from her past, which had come to lose its relation to present circumstance. Such an interpretation collides with the view of Brathwaite, for example, who maintains that the loss of crucial elements of African culture was not voluntary, but imposed by Europeanization and Christianization ("African," 75). The persona affirms, therefore, a double rebellion: against slavery and against the contemporary movement for psychological recuperation of Africa by New World blacks.

The posture assumed here acquires its full meaning when placed in the context of a broader and ongoing Caribbean polemic. In the process of defining national character, there has been considerable debate over the question of whether the Caribbean Negro should affirm an African or a

New World identity. The speaker in this poem assumes the posture of those who emphasize "Caribbeanness." Although she places her origins in Africa, she also makes an explicit effort to avoid rhetorical recuperation of Africa and the putatively atavistic ethos of affirmation of an African identity. In fact, the line "I no longer dreamt of the road to Guinea" is a specific contesting of the desire for reconnection with Africa expressed by Haitian poet Jacques Roumain in his poem "Guinea" (Guinée):

> 'Tis the long road to Guinea
> death will lead you there . . .
> 'Tis the long road to Guinea:
> Where your fathers wait patiently for you. (253)

Morejón's protagonist not only declares her separation from this past, but also demythifies the belief in a single African homeland to which all Afro-Caribbean people belong or can return: "Was it to Guinea? Benin? To Madagascar? Or Cape Verde?" By citing the geographical—and, inferentially, the cultural—distinctions among African peoples, she undercuts the ethnogenetic thrust of black nationalism, which underplays ethnic and cultural differences in order to foment black unity. Like her Francophone counterparts, Morejón deromanticizes Guillén's Afrocentric discourse and displaces the view of Africa as a source of wholeness for Africans in the diaspora.

While the poem seems to eschew the ideology of black nationalism, it contains a strong affirmation of the black woman's *Cuban* nationalism, which was born during slavery. Carlos Moore, a black revisionist of Cuban history, endorses this view in "Cuba: The Untold Story." He attributes the first manifestation of national consciousness in Cuba to the black slaves: "this process of 'Cubanization' on the part of the black slaves, taking place in the midst of the harshest conditions imposed by slavery, did not involve the Spaniards in any way; in other words, the blacks were becoming Afrocubans whereas the whites were remaining Spanish" (182). As we saw in the previous chapter, it is the mulatto woman who has been appropriated as the natural icon of Creole identity, epitomizing, as she does, the racial and cultural conjoining of Africa and Europe. Through the depiction of the black woman in her poem, Morejón offers an alternate Creole icon, defined less by race or cultural identity and more by the firmness of her Cuban roots and commitment.

In the light of this comment, the many verbs that signify work and effort serve to vindicate her claim. This emphasis induces the reader to view the black woman not as a victim, but as a participant in the process of economic production. Tonga Bambé, the slave nanny, found psychic restoration in the joys of vicarious motherhood. In the case of this black female protagonist, her rebirth is constituted by the return on her investment of labor in Cuba since slavery: "And because I worked like an animal / *here* I came to be born" (my emphasis). Her rebirth separates her even further from her African origins and allows her Cuban identity to take root. The emphatic references to her various labor functions also suggest an attitude of defiance in the Afro-Cuban woman, who now claims a central place in the social order, based on her contribution to both economic and political life. It is a strategy that legitimizes her challenge to those who, by perpetuating the system of colonial domination, sought to condemn her to a marginal social position, and also to those who, by stressing her African origins, underestimate or fail to recognize this right.

"Black Woman" reflects the tendency of many contemporary female writers to allow their female characters to represent themselves and interpret their experience. Morejón has chosen a female voice that pretends to speak for all Cuban black women and to embrace their communal history. The image of the Afro-Cuban woman in this poem seems, moreover, to be shaped by a distinct feminist consciousness, which enables the persona to rebel against the dominant male-created images found in other literary works. Some Spanish Caribbean poets who have invested the black woman with political significance have kept her within the stereotypical confines of mothering the black male history-makers. In Morejón's poem, she is not only the subject of the first-person discourse, but she also defines her role as that of political actor. Thus she constructs a counter-model to the literary image of the black woman as aesthetic or sex object.

Historical accounts have either omitted or underplayed the political role of black women in Cuban history. Carlos Moore has been engaged in one of the most spirited campaigns to debunk the white version of Cuban history, but his is a project that involves the use of mainly black male examples to destroy the canon of white founding fathers. Morejón's persona participates in a similar revisionist enterprise, but takes it a step further to displace the "great Man" theory of history. She focuses instead on the political involvement of the anonymous Afro-Cuban woman, who is generally overlooked in the male heroic tradition. This woman is shown as having undertaken various struggles for liberation.

Her resistance begins during slavery and is emblematized in the *palenque*, or runaway slave fort, referred to in line 33. These *palenques* were for a long time the only center of continuing opposition to the colonial regime and of protest against slavery. Morejón condenses the Afro-Cuban woman's participation in the independence struggles of the nineteenth century in the line "and I rode with the troops of Maceo." There is evidence that early in the first war of independence, freedwomen chose to make their contribution through military service rather than through field work. Black peasant women, such as Mariana Grajales, also took part in later stages of the struggle. (See Scott, *Slave Emancipation in Cuba*, and Espín, "The Early Years.") However, the persona's explicit alignment with the Afro-Cuban leader Antonio Maceo is a rejection of that version of Cuban history that has lionized the white "founding fathers" of the independence movement. It is an identification based not merely on race but also on ideology. Antonio Maceo was part of that group of leaders who countered the ideology of white supremacy by espousing the idea of Cuba as a pluralist society in which national patriotism should take precedence over ethnic identity.

Morejón incorporates this issue of female agency into the discourse of "Black Woman" through the semantic nuances in the verb forms. In the first two stanzas the third-person constructions "they made me cross," "they left me here," and "His worship bought me" convey the notion of the black woman's involuntary transplantation from Africa. The counterposed phrase "here I've lived" emphasizes her subsequent adjustment to life in Cuba. Yet this adjustment is not a sign of passivity. All her subsequent responses, indicated by first-person active verbs, represent conscious acts of accommodation or resistance. The view of the Afro-Cuban woman as historical agent extends to her relation to the Revolution. She is not a mere beneficiary of a struggle waged by others, but an active participant in the creation of a new economic, political, and social order.

Two commentaries on this poem have noted its revolutionary import. For Stephanie Davis-Lett the protagonist is a consummate revolutionary figure, not only because of her support for Cuba's socialist transformation, but also because of her rebellion against the traditional images of the black woman (130–31). June Carter also sees this revolutionary stance as the essence of the new image of the black woman projected in the poem (80–81). However, this perceived revolt needs to be placed in the context of Cuban cultural politics. Many Cuban writers, especially in the two decades following the triumph of the Revolution, were committed to the socialist government and frequently used their work to reaffirm its ideology. Consequently, their poetry often assumed a programmatic tone. Even those who did not actively promote socialist theory through literature avoided statements that could be interpreted as counter-revolutionary.

"Black Woman" provides a good illustration of the ideological possibilities and constraints confronting the Cuban artist writing from the official socialist position. It is this ideology that colors the persona's historical vision and admits certain discourses while disallowing others. In this regard, one is reminded of Fidel Castro's 1961 speech "Words to the Intellectuals" (Palabras a los intelectuales), in which he issued the now famous injunction "Within the Revolution, everything; against the Revolution, there are no rights." This idea has set the conceptual parameters within which Morejón writes, and it accounts for the dialectic of transgression and orthodoxy that her depiction of the black woman exemplifies.

On the one hand, Morejón has opened a new terrain for the elaboration of the image of the Afro-Cuban woman. She has moved this woman from the margin to the center of Cuban history. Once voiceless, this woman now speaks with her own voice, thus displacing the male view that has traditionally constituted her as the Other. She presents herself as a social and political actor, rather than as a mere victim of slavery and colonial history. Resistance rather than submission is her natural response to oppression. However, the confinement of this transgression within the limits of revolutionary teaching will be a source of disquiet for many a Caribbean reader. By focusing on the Afro-Cuban woman's adaptation to her new situation, Morejón shows another side of her displacement from Africa. But she realizes this at the cost of some distortion of history; affirmation of her Cuban identity requires de-emphasizing or denial of her links with her African past.

Morejón's posture does not derive from any pure motive. It implies acquiescence with the Cuban Communist Party's alleged discouragement of "separatist" ideologies and "anti-social" practices, such as those of Afro-Cuban religious sects (Moore, "Cuba," 219). In fact, the underlying assumption of the poem seems compatible with the belief expressed by Che Guevara in 1963 that black people in Cuba need to study Marxism-Leninism, not African history (Moore, "Cuba," 217–18). In this poem one receives the impression that, while nationalist sentiments are considered politically legitimate, certain racial sentiments are not. One might even see the poem's title as ironic, since the racial specificity that it anticipates is undercut by the raceless nationalism that the poem espouses. It is obvious, therefore, that not only can revolutionary commitment not share a common ideological space with the strong black consciousness that might be assumed from the title, but it must also override it. Carlos Moore offers a view that competes with this position when he points to the ethnocidal potential (intention?) of such an ideology ("Congo," 12–15).

The persona's pro-Revolution stance is made manifest in her unquestioning acceptance of the assumption of the Castro regime that the new social order has resolved the problems of Cuban blacks. Thus, the Revolution becomes her absolute panacea; it is the means through which she has finally attained an identity ("Now I exist"), an identity that, she implies, is socially and politically constituted, without specific regard to race. It is the remedy for her earlier material deprivation, and the source of liberation of her creative energies ("only today do we own, do we create"). Here the use of the verb "create" is very pointed, for it alludes to the Marxist ideal of nonalienated (creative) labor, achievable under socialism. Unlike the exploitation of her labor under slavery, the achievements and benefits of the Revolution are seen to be commensurate with her material contribution.

According to this version of Cuban history, the Revolution marks both the culmination and the successful conclusion of the black woman's struggles. The egalitarianism claimed, or implied, by the reference to other heirs of the Revolution as "compañeros" further serves to perpetuate the myth that the end of racial prejudice and discrimination is simultaneous with the end of the class struggle. Both the revisionist impulse and the feminist consciousness in this poem are, therefore, subordinated to its dominant imperative: revolutionary ideology. "Black Woman" can be read, on the one hand, as a subversion of established literary and historical discourses. Yet, to the extent that it acquiesces to the assumptions of the Cuban Revolution, and seeks to impose the pro-Revolution interpretation of history, it becomes itself susceptible to a subversive critical reading. Morejón has, in effect, suggested the Afro-Cuban woman's complicity with the writers of the "official" socialist version of her history.

Nicolás Guillén's poem addressed to Angela Davis and published in 1972 reflects more obliquely the ideology of the Cuban Revolution. While Morejón fashions a new image out of material available in Cuban history, Guillén chooses to focus on a well-known African American political activist. Like Morejón, Guillén recognized the need to develop new models of the woman of African descent. But he replaced the implicit transgression of her poem with an open announcement of a break with earlier convention:

I have not come here to tell you that you are beautiful.
I think that you are, that you are beautiful,
but that is not the reason . . .
Angela, I do not stand before your name
to speak to you of love like an adolescent,
nor to desire you like a satyr.
Oh, that is not the reason. (qtd. in Morales, 369)

Guillén's refusal to promote Davis's aesthetic and sexual attributes signals his rejection of the dominant stereotypes that the male imagination has created. He highlights instead spiritual strength and political courage as her defining characteristics:

You are made of a rough, shiny metal,
an impetus that will not rust,
strong enough to withstand
the sun and the rain,
the wind and the moon
and the storm. (qtd. in Morales, 369)

Guillén's selection of this African American woman is significant on two levels. First, it is an index of the poet's tendency after the 1940s to focus on the interconnection of local and international political causes. Second, he invests a historical personality and her experience with symbolic importance, unlike the earlier nationalists, who had appropriated an abstract *mulata* figure as their ideological symbol.

Even the connotative function of the imagery in Guillén's poem reflects this shift in perspective. The metal imagery in the last quotation may be compared with Muñoz del Monte's use of bronze as a metaphor to characterize the *mulata*. In that instance bronze symbolized racial duality. Guillén, however, gives new value to this image, using it to allude to Davis's spiritual strength rather than her physical properties. He emphasizes her role as historical agent:

You are strong and plastic, I say,
you can jump to (and break) the neck of those who want, have
    wanted
and will want forever
to see you burnt alive tied to the south of our country.
. . . .

The enemy is clumsy.
He wants to silence your voice with his voice, but we all know
    that
yours is the only voice that echoes,
the only one that burns
high in the night like a lightning column. (qtd. in Morales, 370)

One feature of the representation of women's condition under patriarchy, which feminist critics have noted, is the use of silence or the repression of words to connote oppression. Seen in this context, the poet's focus on Angela Davis's voice is not coincidental. Christopher Miller has observed that "politically, the voice remains our central metaphor for political agency and power" and that "having a voice means empowerment" (*Theories*, 248). Davis's voice acquires metonymic and metaphorical value, signifying both her ideological stance and her external expression of her political resistance. Because of her prominent involvement in the struggle for social justice, the poet can invoke this figure as an ideologically appropriate model of black womanhood in the context of contemporary Cuban political reality.

These two poets responded to the ideological imperatives of the moment by using an explicitly or implicitly pro-Revolution discourse to create their images. In the emerging literature of the Cuban diaspora, the Afro-Cuban woman also features in anti-revolutionary discourse. While Morejón wishes her to be seen as the unequivocal beneficiary of the revolution, the following two poems, published anonymously by Cuban expatriates, present a more skeptical vision of her experience of revolutionary change.

Political satire in "Now I Am a Member of the Women's Federation" (Ahora yo soy federá) undercuts the triumphant climax with which Morejón ends her account of the Afro-Cuban woman's journey:

before Fidel I was a poor black woman.
I lived in Arroyo Apolo, in a room in a tenement yard,
but now I am living in a chalet in Miramar.
We have no chairs to sit on, no water to wash
but that does not matter, my friend, now I live in Miramar.
That progress is because I am in the Women's Federation.
Besides I work at the National Bank;
I sign with a cross, but in a few months
when I learn how to sign
they will give me a diploma saying "Literate"

and they'll promote me to cashier . . . you'll see, Caridá
. . . .
At night I go dancing at the Social Circle
in the same ballrooms where the big shots used to dance
Julio Losbo, Gosme Mena, the Apuros and the Menocás;
It's a pity that without shoes dancing is dangerous.
I must look after those I've got, because for six months, my friend
they'll not sell me another pair . . . that I won't get
though I'm in the Federation.
Poor Misdali, how I pity her,
she is still foolish, she won't join the Federation
poor blockhead living in a tenement yard.
She'll always be black, forever and ever.
But I get better every day;
I go to hear Lázaro Peña's talk,
I talk with Fidel Castro, I go to the University
to get my Worker's Certificate and to learn to sign my name;
I'm a member of the Defense Committee, do weekly guard duty,
on Sundays I cut cane or pick coffee.
Never mind that I'm so skinny . . .
and I'm hardly eating . . . and not for want of appetite
Look all around . . . No one's listening, Caridad
Hey, listen my dear . . . I CAN'T TAKE IT NO MORE
FOR A PIECE OF HAM I WOULD LEAVE THE FEDERATION. (qtd. in Ruiz
    del Vizo, Poesía, 17–18)

Here the criticism of the Revolution is transmitted indirectly through
irony; the woman's final declaration serves to erode all the preceding assertions about the gains of the Revolution, betraying the insincerity of her
claims of contentment and social improvement and her lack of real commitment to revolutionary politics.

The black speaker of "Black Woman Duped" (La negra equivocá) is used
to make a more direct anti-revolutionary statement:

1959, year of the Revolution.
The year on which the Cuban people set their hopes.
A black woman sat thinking, not too deeply
and she thought more about what the Revolution would bring
Oh yes! Now it's all over
this business of not entering the "Ten Cent" and "El Encanto"
Of course not! Now this black woman

can surely come and go as she pleases
for all that belongs to the people now

. . . .

I'll eat ham, suckling pig
and all that the Agrarian Reform will bring . . .
I'll learn to drive and I'll drive all through the capital
Oh my dear! At last I'll live like a queen . . .
But since everything in life passes and everything must pass
comes the year 1964 and "The Black Woman she's Mistaken.

. . . .

Oh! I do not know what's wrong with me, three years have passed
and the black woman is still the same,
eating rice and beans (they call it *seguimiento*).
To the Tropicana, to the Capri, to the Social Circle
this black woman has never been.
And I believe that play basketball she never will.
(qtd. in González-Pérez, *Poesía,* 10–12)

The voices of these working-class black women contest the version of
events offered by the persona of Morejón's poem. Counterpoint is a standard technique used by many writers who support the Cuban Revolution.
Their juxtaposition of past deprivation and oppression with present advances is used typically for favorable evaluation of the Castro regime.
These two poems have also employed the technique of counterpoint to
explore the relationship between the past and the present social conditions
of the Afro-Cuban woman, but subversively; they foreground the discrepancy between promise and realization, between expectation and achievement, between overt expression and underlying reality.

Also contrasting with the carefully contrived structure and the formal-
ity of the language of "Black Woman" is the popular speech of these two
poems. Despite the difference in modality, however, the ideological content and intention of the last two are of no less significance than they are
in the first. The choice of speakers who record their lived experience of
revolutionary society add persuasive power to these poems' demythi-
fication of the image of the Afro-Cuban woman that pro-Revolution
rhetoric produces in Morejón's poem. However, the significant development manifested by all three examples is that the black woman has moved
from being the mere subject of a poetic discourse to becoming the spokes-
person for a specific ideological position.

Conclusion

A history of subjugation sets in motion a process
of its own negation: a history of resistance.
NGUGI WA THIONGO

For the convenience of analysis, I have chosen in this book to separate the different dimensions of the literary representations of Afro-Caribbean women. This, however, does not obscure the fact that these images are the products of an intricate interplay of sex, gender, color, social class, and history. The representations have more than intrinsic value. They give an indication of how some Caribbean writers have interpreted historical change. Refracted in them are the varied responses of Caribbean people to important developments in their history. In the representational process the Afro-Caribbean woman has been a virtual blank text on which writers have inscribed important highlights, if not the whole process of the region's modern history. The nineteenth-century images transmit the social interactions and race relations of slave society and the colonial period, while the twentieth-century representations bespeak the vicissitudes of the journey toward independence.

Since history shapes both the vision and the expression of the writers, a certain correlation also exists between the historical-ideological contexts and the literary discourses. Nineteenth-century writers viewed the Afro-Caribbean woman, by and large, through European lenses and depicted her through the use of European conventions. But even in this earlier period a certain inclination to modify the inherited discourse was discernible. Dependence diminishes with the awakening of nationalist consciousness and the desire to define a Caribbean self.

The foregoing analysis does not constitute a demand for positive literary images of Afro-Caribbean women. It has probed some of the complexities and the problems of the domain of Caribbean literary discourse to establish the status of these images as representations and considered their effects and implications. For example, the aesthetic discourse that centers on color reinforces the impossibility of arriving at a monolithic aesthetic standard in racially diverse societies such as the Caribbean and establishes the need to recognize and accommodate diverse aesthetic forms. The images do not merely reflect but can also influence the way real black and mulatto women are perceived and treated. Encoded in the representations are not merely the perceptions of their creators, but also their projections of conscious and unconscious desires and ideologies. Their significance lies as much in what they tell us about Afro-Caribbean women and their position in society as in what they tell us about the image-makers and their fantasies.

It is evident that many Spanish Caribbean writers have been concerned with vindicating the Afro-Caribbean woman and validating her contribution to Caribbean cultural life. They are just as evidently concerned with presenting enlightened self-images. However, this enterprise can be vitiated when the dominant ideology proves resistant to efforts to create an alternative discourse. Very common, and perhaps indicative of the discomfort that they feel in dealing with the subject, are the examples of writers whose residual and subliminal prejudice aborts their redemptive projects, or who create images that do not so much vindicate as they further objectify and demean the woman of African descent.

One crucial determinant of literary vision and its expression is the position of the writer. Many, especially those of the earlier period, wrote about the black or mulatto woman from the perspective of the dominant culture. Their work evinced the distance separating them from their subjects. Such a distance is apparent in the recurrence of poems that differentiate the Afro-Caribbean woman through the use of racial or sexual criteria. It underpins the construction of difference as deviation from, or inferiority to, the norms of the dominant white-oriented culture.

It is a distance that helps to account for the discrepancy between motive and effect. Many of the early attempts to speak on behalf of these women or to view them from the inside failed to achieve that intention. It is important to recognize the positive motivations of writers who express through their work their resistance to alien and alienating modes of representation of people of African ancestry. Their desire to foster positive self-images in people of African descent, and to bring about their social redemption, is undeniable. But literary efforts to redeem or canonize the Afro-Caribbean woman or to rehabilitate her image have frequently served to obscure as much as to illuminate her reality. In the worst instances these efforts have served to perpetuate the very notions the writers set out to negate.

The kind of critical scrutiny to which the poems have been submitted illustrates the dynamic and dialogic nature of the field of literary discourse. According to Mikhail Bakhtin, "a word, discourse, language or culture undergoes dialogization when it becomes relativized, de-privileged, aware of competing definitions for the same things. Undialogized language is authoritative or absolute" (427). The image-making process that has been the subject of this study is characterized by ideological heterogeneity rather than uniformity. Ideologies contend with each other; each new discourse appears to be engaging with a prevailing or preceding discourse; the terms of engagement imply either complicity or opposition.

In many instances, it has been possible to view the writers as agents of ideological practice, acting to ensure the predominance of the cultural norms, values, and ideas of the dominant class over the dominated (Woolcock, 204). Their definitions of the Afro-Caribbean woman serve to legitimize her subordinate status and even to rationalize discriminatory or inhuman treatment. In these cases, their definitions collide with the perspectives of those who resist or question prevailing beliefs, who express implicit protest against the social condition of these women, or who have generated a counter-discourse to vindicate the woman of African descent. And it is this oppositional role that is the most vital, since it is the one that produces new visions and alternate modes of representation.

BIBLIOGRAPHY

Albornoz, Aurora de, and Julio Rodríguez Luis, eds. *Sensemayá: La poesía negra en el mundo hispanoamericano.* Madrid: Editoriales Orígenes, 1980.

Alcántara Almánzar, José. *Estudios de poesía dominicana.* Santo Domingo: Editora Alfa y Omega, 1979.

Allfrey, Phyllis Shand. *The Orchid House.* New York: E. P. Dutton, 1954.

Althusser, Louis. *Lenin and Philosophy and Other Essays.* London: New Left Books, 1977.

Argüedas, Alcides. *Pueblo enfermo.* Barcelona: Editorial Vda. de Luis Tasso, 1911.

Arnedo, Miguel. "The Portrayal of the Afro-Cuban Female Dancer in Cuban *Negrista* Poetry." *Afro-Hispanic Review* 16, no. 2 (1997): 26–33.

Arnold, A. James. *Modernism and Négritude: The Poetry and Poetics of Aimé Césaire.* Cambridge, Mass.: Harvard University Press, 1981.

Arozarena, Marcelino. *Canción negra sin color.* 1966; rpt. Nendeln, Germany: Kraus, 1970.

Arrom, José Juan. "La poesía afrocubana." *Revista iberoamericana* 4 (1942): 379–411.

———. "Presencia del negro en la poesía folklórica americana." In *Certidumbre de América,* 122–53. Madrid: Editorial Gredos, 1971.

Bakhtin, M. M. *The Dialogic Imagination.* Trans. Caryl Emerson and M. Holquist. Austin: University of Texas Press, 1981.

Ballagas, Emilio. *Elegía sin nombre.* 1930; rpt. Havana: Editorial Letras Cubanas, 1981.

———. *Mapa de la poesía negra americana.* 1946; rpt. Nendeln, Germany: Kraus, 1970.

———. "Situación de la poesía afro-americana." In *Iniciación a la poesía afro-americana,* edited by Oscar Fernández de la Vega and Alberto Pamies, 37–77. Miami: Ediciones Universal, 1973.

Balseiro, Isabel. "Through the Looking Glass Darkly: Rosario Ferré's 'Cuando las mujeres quieren a los hombres'." *Afro-Hispanic Review* 16, no. 2 (1997): 3–9.

Bar-Lewaw, Itzhak. *Plácido: Vida y obra.* Mexico: Ediciones Botas, 1960.

Barnet, Miguel. *Biografía de un cimarrón.* Havana: Instituto de Etnología y Folklore, 1966.

Baugh, Edward. *West Indian Poetry, 1900–1970: A Study in Cultural Decolonization.* Kingston, Jamaica: Savacou Publications, n.d.

Beane, Carol. "*Mestizaje:* 'Civilization' or 'Barbarie': Prospects for Cultural Continuity in *Matalache, Pobre negro,* and *Cumboto.*" *Studies in Afro-Hispanic Literature* 3 (1979): 199–212.

Beckles, Hilary. *Afro-Caribbean Women and Resistance to Slavery in Barbados.* London: Karnak House, 1988.

———. *Natural Rebels: A Social History of Enslaved Black Women in Barbados.* New Brunswick: Rutgers University Press, 1989.

Belsey, Catherine. *Critical Practice.* London: Methuen, 1980.

Betts, Raymond F. *The Ideology of Blackness.* Lexington, Mass.: D. C. Heath, 1971.

Blomberg, Hector Pedro. "La negra y la mulata en la poesía americana." *Atenea* 53 (1945): 4–21.

Boulware, Kay. "Woman and Nature in *Negrismo.*" *Studies in Afro-Hispanic Literature* 1 (1977): 16–25.

Boyce Davies, Carole, and Elaine Savory Fido, eds. *Out of the Kumbla: Caribbean Women and Literature.* Trenton, N.J.: Africa World Press, 1990.

Brathwaite, Edward. "The African Presence in Caribbean Literature." In *Slavery, Colonialism, and Racism,* edited by Sidney W. Mintz, 73–109. New York: W. W. Norton, 1974.

———. "Creative Literature of the British West Indies during the Period of Slavery." *Savacou* 1 (1970): 46–73.

Brodber, Erna. *Perceptions of Caribbean Women: Toward a Documentation of Stereotypes.* Cave Hill, Barbados: Institute of Social and Economic Research, 1982.

Burnett, Paula, ed. *The Penguin Book of Caribbean Verse in English.* New York: Penguin, 1986.

Bush, Barbara. *Slave Women in Caribbean Society (1650–1838).* London: James Curry, 1990.

———. "White 'Ladies,' Coloured 'Favourites,' and Black 'Wenches': Some Considerations on Sex, Race, and Class Factors in Social Relations in White Creole Society in the British Caribbean." *Slavery and Abolition* 2 (1981): 245–62.

Calcagno, Francisco. *Los crímenes de Concha.* Havana: Librería e Imprenta de Elías F. Casona, 1887.

———. *Romualdo: Uno de tantos.* In *Noveletas Cubanas.* 1864, 1884; rpt. Havana: Editorial de Arte y Literatura, 1974.

Campbell, George. *First Poems.* Kingston, Jamaica: n.p., 1945.

Carter, June. "La Negra as Metaphor in Afro–Latin American Poetry." *Caribbean Quarterly* 31 (1985): 73–82.

Cartey, Wilfred. *Black Images.* New York: Teachers College Press, Columbia University, 1970.

Castillo, Debra A. *Talking Back: Toward a Latin American Feminist Literary Criticism.* Ithaca: Cornell University Press, 1992.

Christian, Barbara. *Black Feminist Criticism.* Oxford: Pergamon Press, 1985.

Clytus, John. *Black Man in Red Cuba.* Coral Gables: University of Miami Press, 1970.

Cobham-Sander, Rhonda. "Women in Jamaican Literature, 1900–1950." In *Out of the Kumbla: Caribbean Women and Literature,* edited by Carole Boyce Davies and Elaine Savory Fido, 195–222. Trenton, N.J.: Africa World Press, 1990.

Colón Pellot, Carmen. *Ambar mulato (Ritmos).* Arecibo, P.R.: n.p., 1938.

Congreso de literatura afroamericana. *Homenaje a Lydia Cabrera.* Miami: Ediciones Universal, 1978.

Cornejo-Parriego, Rosalía. "Racialización colonial y diferencia feminina en 'Love Story' de Poniatowska y 'Cuando las mujeres quieren a los hombres' de Ferré." *Afro-Hispanic Review* 16, no. 2 (1997): 10–18.

Cornejo Polar, Antonio. "El indigenismo y las literaturas heterogéneas: Su doble estatuto socio-cultural." *Revista de crítica literaria latinoamericana* 4, nos. 7–8 (1978): 7–21.

Coulthard, G. R. "Parallelisms and Divergencies between 'Négritude' and 'Indigenismo'." *Caribbean Studies* 8 (1968): 31–55.

———. *Race and Colour in Caribbean Literature.* Oxford: Oxford University Press, 1962.

———. "The Situation of the Writer in Contemporary Cuba." *Caribbean Studies* 7 (1967): 23–35.

———, ed. *Caribbean Literature: An Anthology.* London: University of London Press, 1966.

Cudjoe, Selwyn R. *Resistance and Caribbean Literature.* Athens: Ohio University Press, 1980.

———, ed. *Caribbean Women Writers.* Wellesley, Mass.: Calaloux Publications, 1990.

Dash, J. Michael. *Haiti and the United States.* London: Macmillan, 1988.

Dathorne, O. R. *Caribbean Verse.* London: Heinemann, 1967.

———. *Dark Ancestor.* Baton Rouge: Louisiana State University Press, 1981.

Davis, James J. "On Black Poetry in the Dominican Republic." *Afro-Hispanic Review* 1, no. 3 (1982): 27–30.

Davis, Paul. "The Black Man and the Caribbean as Seen by Nicolás Guillén and Luis Palés Matos." *Caribbean Quarterly* 25 (1979): 72–79.

Davis-Lett, Stephanie. "The Image of the Black Woman as a Revolutionary Figure: Three Views." *Studies in Afro-Hispanic Literature* 2–3 (1978–79): 118–31.

DeCosta, Miriam, ed. *Blacks in Hispanic Literature: Critical Essays.* Port Washington, N.Y.: Kennikat Press, 1977.

DeCosta-Willis, Miriam. "Self and Society in the Afro-Cuban Slave Narrative." *Latin American Literary Review* 16 (1978): 6–15.

Del Cabral, Manuel. *Historia de mi voz.* Chile: Ediciones Andes, 1964.

DeLisser, H. G. *Psyche.* London: Macmillan, 1980.

Drayton, Arthur. "West Indian Consciousness in West Indian Verse." *Journal of Commonwealth Literature* 9 (1970): 66–88.

Eagleton, Terry. *Literary Theory: An Introduction.* Minneapolis: University of Minnesota Press, 1983.

Easthope, Anthony. *Poetry as Discourse.* London: Methuen, 1983.

Edwards, Bryan. *The History of the British Colonies in the West Indies.* Vol. 2. London, 1801.

Ellis, Keith. *Cuba's Nicolás Guillén: Poetry and Ideology.* Toronto: University of Toronto Press, 1983.

Espín, Vilma. "The Early Years." In *Women and the Cuban Revolution,* edited by Elizabeth Stone, 33–46. New York: Pathfinder Press, 1981.

Fanon, Frantz. *Black Skin, White Mask.* Trans. Charles Markmann. New York: Grove Press, 1967.

———. *The Wretched of the Earth.* New York: Penguin, 1967.

Ferguson, Moira, ed. *The History of Mary Prince, a West Indian Slave, Related by Herself.* London: Pandora, 1987.

Fernández de la Vega, Oscar, and Alberto Pamies, eds. *Iniciación a la poesía afroamericana.* Miami: Ediciones Universal, 1973.

Fernández Spencer, Antonio. *Nueva poesía dominicana.* Madrid: Ediciones Cultura Hispánica, 1953.

Ferré, Rosario. *Papeles de Pandora.* Mexico: Joaquín Mortíz, 1976.

Figueroa, John, ed. *Caribbean Voices: An Anthology of West Indian Poetry.* Vol. 1. London: Evans Brothers, 1968.

Fivel-Démoret, Sharon. "La belle ou la bête: La femme noire dans le roman cubain du 19ème siècle." *Actes du Colloque "Canne à Sucre et Littérature dans la Caraibe et l'Océan Indien."* Martinique: Association Populaire pour l'Education Scientifique/Centre Régional de Documentation Pédagogique, 1991.

———. "The Production and Consumption of Propaganda Literature: The Cuban Anti-Slavery Novel." *Bulletin of Hispanic Studies* 66 (1989): 1–12.

Foster, David William. *Cuban Literature: A Research Guide.* New York: Garland, 1985.

———. *Puerto Rican Literature: A Bibliography of Secondary Sources.* Westport, Conn.: Greenwood Press, 1982.

Foucault, Michel. "Orders of Discourse." *Social Science Information* 10, no. 2 (1971): 7–30.

Foulkes, A. P. *Literature and Propaganda.* London: Methuen, 1983.

———. *The Search for Literary Meaning.* Bern, Switzerland: H. Lang, 1975.

Fowler, Roger. *Linguistics and the Novel.* London: Methuen, 1977.

———. *Literature as Social Discourse.* London: Batsford Academic and Educational, 1981.

————. "Power." In *Handbook of Discourse Analysis*. Vol. 4. Edited by Teun A. van Dijk, 61–82. Orlando, Fla.: Academic Press, 1985.

Franco, J. L. *La presencia negra en el nuevo mundo*. Havana: Casa de las Américas, 1968.

Fredrickson, George M. *The Black Image in the White Mind*. New York: Harper and Row, 1971.

Gilman, Sander. "Black Bodies, White Bodies: Toward an Iconography of Female Sexuality in Late Nineteenth-Century Art, Medicine, and Literature." *Critical Inquiry* 12 (1985): 204–42.

González, José Emilio. "Tres danzas negras de Luis Palés Matos." *Asomante* 25, no. 4 (1969): 20–33.

González, José Luis, and Mónica Mansour, eds. *Poesía negra de América*. Mexico: Ediciones Era, 1976.

González-Pérez, Armando. *Antología clave de la poesía afroamericana*. Madrid: Ediciones Alcalá, 1976.

————. *Poesía afrocubana última*. Milwaukee: University of Wisconsin Center for Latin America, 1975.

————. "Raza y eros en la poesía afrocubana de Nicolás Guillén." *Homenaje a Lydia Cabrera*. Congreso de literatura afroamericana. Miami: Ediciones Universal, 1977.

Guillén, Nicolás. *Obra poética*. 2 vols. Havana: Editorial de Arte y Literatura, 1974.

Guirao, Ramón. *Orbita de la poesía afrocubana, 1928–1937 (Antología)*. 1938; rpt. Nendeln, Germany: Kraus, 1970.

Hays, H. R. *The Dangerous Sex: The Myth of Feminine Evil*. New York: Pocket Books, 1966.

Helg, Aline. *Our Rightful Share: The Afro-Cuban Struggle for Equality, 1886–1912*. Chapel Hill: University of North Carolina Press, 1995.

Hodge, Merle. *Crick Crack, Monkey*. London: Heinemann, 1981.

Hoetink, H. *The Two Variants in Caribbean Race Relations*. Trans. Eva M. Hooykaas. London: Oxford University Press, 1967.

Hoffmann, Léon-François. *Essays on Haitian Literature*. Washington, D.C.: Three Continents Press, 1984.

Hunsaker, Steven V. "Representing the *mulata: El amor en los tiempos de cólera* and *Tenda dos Milagres*." *Hispania* 77 (1994): 225–34.

Instituto de Literatura y Lingüística de la Academia de Ciencias de Cuba. *Perfil histórico de las letras cubanas desde los orígenes hasta 1898*. Havana: Editorial Letras Cubanas, 1983.

Irish, George. "Nicolás Guillén's Position on Race: A Reappraisal." *Revista/Review Interamericana* 6 (1976): 335–47.

Jackson, Richard L. *The Afro-Spanish American Author: An Annotated Bibliography*. New York: Garland, 1980.

————. *The Black Image in Latin American Literature*. Albuquerque: University of New Mexico Press, 1976.

————. *Black Writers in Latin America.* Albuquerque: University of New Mexico Press, 1979.

————. "Literary Blackness and Literary Americanism: Toward an Afro Model for Latin American Literature." *Afro-Hispanic Review* 1, no. 2 (1982): 5–11.

————. "La presencia negra en la obra de Rubén Darío." *Revista iberoamericana* 33, no. 64 (1967): 395–417.

————. "Research on Black Themes in Spanish American Literature: A Bibliographic Guide to Recent Trends." *Latin American Research Review* 12 (1977): 87–103.

Jahn, Janheinz. *A History of Neo-African Literature.* London: Faber and Faber, 1968.

Johnson, Lemuel A. *The Devil, The Gargoyle, and The Buffoon: The Negro as Metaphor in Western Literature.* Port Washington, N.Y.: Kennikat Press, 1971.

————. "*El Tema Negro:* The Nature of Primitivism in the Poetry of Luis Palés Matos." In *Blacks in Hispanic Literature: Critical Essays,* edited by Miriam DeCosta, 123–36. Port Washington, N.Y.: Kennikat Press, 1977.

King, Bruce, ed. *West Indian Literature.* London: Macmillan, 1979.

Knight, Vere. "French-Caribbean Literature: A Literature of Commitment." *Revista interamericana* 5 (1975): 67–92.

Kress, Gunther. "Ideological Structures in Discourse." In *Handbook of Discourse Analysis.* Vol. 4. Edited by Teun A. van Dijk, 27–42. Orlando, Fla.: Academic Press, 1985.

Kutzinski, Vera M. *Sugar's Secrets: Race and the Erotics of Cuban Nationalism.* Charlottesville: University of Virginia Press, 1993.

Latortue, Régine. "Le discourse de la nature: La Femme noire dans la littérature häitienne." *Notre Libraire* 73 (1984): 65–69.

Lewis, Gordon K. *Main Currents in Caribbean Thought.* Baltimore: Johns Hopkins University Press, 1983.

Lewis, Marvin A. *Afro-Hispanic Poetry, 1940–1980: From Slavery to "Négritude" in South American Verse.* Columbia: University of Missouri Press, 1983.

Lloréns Torres, Luis. *Obras completas.* Vol. 1. San Juan, P.R.: Instituto de Cultura Puertorriqueña, 1967.

Luis, William. *Voices from Under: Black Narrative in Latin America and the Caribbean.* Westport, Conn.: Greenwood Press, 1984.

Mansour, Mónica. *La poesía negrista.* Mexico: Ediciones Era, 1973.

Manuel, Peter. *Caribbean Currents: Caribbean Music from Rumba to Reggae.* Philadelphia: Temple University Press, 1995.

Manzano, Juan Francisco. *Autobiografía, cartas y versos de Juan Francisco Manzano.* Ed. José L. Franco. Havana: Municipio de la Habana, 1937.

Márquez, Robert. "Zombi to Synthesis: Notes on the Negro in Spanish American Literature." *Jamaica Journal* 11 (1977): 22–31.

Márquez, Robert, and David Arthur McMurray, trans. *Man-Making Words: Selected Poems of Nicolás Guillén.* Havana: Editorial de Arte y Literatura, 1973.

Mathurin, Lucille. *The Rebel Woman in the British West Indies during Slavery.* Kingston, Jamaica: Institute of Jamaica, 1975.

Matthews, Thomas G. "The Question of Color in Puerto Rico." In *Slavery and Race Relations in Latin America,* edited by Robert Brent Toplin, 299–323. Westport, Conn.: Greenwood Press, 1974.

McKay, Claude. *Harlem Shadows.* New York: Harcourt, Brace, 1922.

Megenny, William W. "The Black in Hispanic-Caribbean and Brazilian Poetry: A Comparative Perspective." *Revista interamericana* 5 (1975): 47–66.

Mellafe, Rolando. *Negro Slavery in Latin America.* Trans. J. W. S. Judge. Berkeley: University of California Press, 1975.

Melón, Alfred. *Realidad, poesia e ideología.* Havana: Ediciones Union, 1973.

Méndez, José Luis. *Para una sociología de la literatura puertorriqueña.* Havana: Casa de las Américas, 1982.

Miller, Christopher, L. *Blank Darkness: Africanist Discourse in French.* Chicago: University of Chicago Press, 1985.

———. *Theories of Africans: Francophone Literature and Anthropology in Africa.* Chicago: University of Chicago Press, 1990.

Minc, Rose S., ed. *Literatures in Transition: The Many Voices of the Caribbean Area.* Montclair, N.J.: Montclair State College, 1982.

Mintz, Sidney W., ed. *Slavery, Colonialism, and Racism.* New York: W. W. Norton, 1974.

Mitchell, Juliet. *Woman's Estate.* New York: Pantheon Books, 1972.

Monguió, Luis. "El negro en algunos poetas españoles y americanos anteriores a 1800." *Revista Iberoamericana* 22 (1957): 245–59.

Moore, Carlos. *Castro, the Blacks, and Africa.* Los Angeles: Center for Afro-American Studies, University of California, 1988.

———. "Congo or Carabalí? Race Relations in Socialist Cuba." *Caribbean Review* 15, no. 2 (1986): 12–15.

———. "Cuba: The Untold Story." *Présence Africaine* (English ed.) 52 (1964): 117–229.

Morales, Jorge Luis, ed. *Poesía afroantillana y negrista (Puerto Rico, República Dominicana, Cuba).* Río Piedras, P.R.: Editorial Universitaria, 1976.

Mordecai, Pamela, and Elizabeth Wilson, eds. *Her True-True Name: An Anthology of Women's Writing from the Caribbean.* Jamaica: Heinemann, 1989.

Morejón, Nancy. "Mujer negra." *Casa de las Américas* 88 (1975): 119–20.

———. *Nación y mestizaje en Nicolás Guillén.* Havana: Unión de Escritores y Artistas de Cuba, 1982.

———, ed. *Recopilación de textos sobre Nicolás Guillén.* Havana: Casa de las Américas, 1974.

Morris, Mervyn, ed. *Seven Jamaican Poets.* Kingston, Jamaica: Bolivar Press, 1971.

Nettleford, Rex. *Identity, Race, and Protest in Jamaica.* New York: William Morrow, 1972.

Noble, Enrique. "Ethnic and Social Aspects of Negro Poetry of Latin America." *Phylon Quarterly* 18 (1957): 391–401.

———. *Literatura afro-hispanoamericana*. Lexington, Mass.: Xerox College Publishing, 1973.

O'Callaghan, Evelyn. *Woman Version: Theoretical Approaches to West Indian Fiction by Women*. New York: Macmillan, 1993.

Olivera, Otto. "La mujer de color en la poesía de Nicolás Guillén." *Homenaje a Lydia Cabrera*. Congreso de literatura afroamericana, 165–73. Miami: Ediciones Universal, 1977.

Ortiz, Fernando. *Los negros esclavos*. 1916; rpt. Havana: Editorial de Ciencias Sociales, 1975.

———. "Los últimos versos mulatos." 1935; rpt. *Iniciación a la poesía afroamericana*, edited by Oscar Fernández de la Vega and Alberto Pamies, 156–71. Miami: Ediciones Universal, 1973.

Otero, Lisandro. *En ciudad semejante*. Havana: Ediciones Unión de Escritores y Artistas de Cuba, 1970.

———. *La situación*. Havana: Casa de las Américas, 1963.

Palés Matos, Luis. *Poesía completa y prosa selecta*. Caracas: Biblioteca Ayacucho, 1978.

Patterson, Orlando. *The Sociology of Slavery*. London: Granada Publishing, 1973.

Pereda Valdéz, Ildefonso. *Lo negro y lo mulato en la poesía cubana*. Montevideo: Ediciones Ciudadela, 1970.

Rhys, Jean. *Wide Sargasso Sea*. 1966; rpt. New York: Norton, 1982.

Rodríguez, Ileana, and Marc Zimmerman, eds. *Process of Unity in Caribbean Society: Ideologies and Literature*. Minneapolis: Institute for the Study of Hispanic and Luso-Brazilian Literature, 1983.

Rodríguez, María Cristina. "Poor-Black, Rich-White: Women in *La guaracha del macho Camacho*." *Studies in Afro-Hispanic Literature* 3 (1979): 244–54.

Roumain, Jacques. *La montagne ensorcelée*. Paris: Les Editeurs Français Réunis, 1972.

Rout, Leslie B. *The African Experience in Spanish America*. Cambridge: Cambridge University Press, 1976.

Ruiz del Vizo, Hortensia. *Black Poetry of the Americas (A Bilingual Anthology)*. Miami: Ediciones Universal, 1972.

———. *Poesía negra del Caribe y otras áreas*. Miami: Ediciones Universal, 1972.

Saakana, Amon S. *The Colonial Legacy in Caribbean Literature*. Trenton, N.J.: Africa World Press, 1987.

Said, Edward. *Orientalism*. New York: Pantheon Books, 1978.

Sarmiento, Domingo F. *Facundo*. Buenos Aires: Losada, 1963.

Scott, Rebecca. *Slave Emancipation in Cuba*. Princeton: Princeton University Press, 1985.

Seidel, Gill. "Political Discourse Analysis." In *Handbook of Discourse Analysis*. Vol. 4. Edited by Teun A. van Dijk, 43–60. Orlando, Fla.: Academic Press, 1985.

Shapiro, N., ed. *Négritude: Black Poetry from Africa and the Caribbean.* New York: October House, 1970.

Shelton, Marie-Denise. "Women Writers of the French-Speaking Caribbean: An Overview." In *Caribbean Women Writers*, edited by Selwyn R. Cudjoe, 346–56. Wellesley, Mass.: Calaloux Publications, 1990.

Smart, Ian I. "*Mulatez* and the Image of the Black *mujer nueva* in Guillén's Poetry." *Kentucky Romance Quarterly* 29 (1982): 379–90.

———. *Nicolás Guillén, Popular Poet of the Caribbean.* Columbia: University of Missouri Press, 1990.

Smith, Paul Julian. *Representing the Other: 'Race,' Text, and Gender in Spanish and Spanish American Narrative.* Oxford: Clarendon Press, 1992.

Smith, R. T. "People and Change." *New World* 2 (1966): 49–54.

Smorkaloff, Pamela María. *If I Could Write This in Fire: An Anthology of Literature from the Caribbean.* New York: New Press, 1994.

Stimson, Frederick. *The New Schools of Spanish American Poetry.* Chapel Hill: University of North Carolina Press, 1970.

Stone, Elizabeth, ed. *Women and the Cuban Revolution.* New York: Pathfinder Press, 1981.

Suárez y Romero, Anselmo. *Francisco.* 1880; rpt. Havana: Cuadernos de Cultura, 1947.

Tanco y Bosmoniel, Felix M. *Petrona y Rosalía.* 1838; rpt. Havana: Editorial Letras Cubanas, 1980.

Thomas, Hugh. *Cuba: The Pursuit of Freedom.* New York: Harper and Row, 1971.

Tiffany, Sharon W., and Kathleen J. Adams. *The Wild Woman: An Inquiry into the Anthropology of an Idea.* Cambridge, Mass.: Schenkman Publishing, 1985.

Torres-Saillant, Silvio. *Caribbean Poetics: Toward an Aesthetic of West Indian Literature.* Cambridge: Cambridge University Press, 1997.

Valdés, Gabriel de la Concepción. *Los poemas más representativos de Plácido (Edición crítica).* Introd. Frederick S. Stimson and Humberto E. Robles. Chapel Hill: University of North Carolina Press, 1976.

Valdés-Cruz, Rosa E. *La poesía negroide en América.* New York: Las Americas Publishing, 1970.

———. "Tres poemas representativos de la poesía afroantillana." *Hispania* 54, no. 1 (March 1970): 39–45.

Van Dijk, Teun A. *Prejudice in Discourse: An Analysis of Ethnic Prejudice in Cognition and Conversation.* Amsterdam: John Benjamins Publishing, 1984.

———, ed. *Handbook of Discourse Analysis.* 4 vols. Orlando, Fla.: Academic Press, 1985.

Vaughan, H. A. *Sandy Lane and Other Poems.* Bridgetown, Barbados: Bim, 1985.

Villaverde, Cirilo. *Cecilia Valdés.* 2 vols. 1839 and 1882; rpt. Havana: Instituto Cubano del libro, 1972.

Vitier, Cintio. *Lo cubano en la poesía.* Havana: Instituto Cubano del libro, 1970.

Walcott, Derek. *Another Life.* New York: Farrar, Straus, and Giroux, 1972.

Weaver, Kathleen. *Where the Island Sleeps Like a Wing.* San Francisco: Black Scholar Press, 1985.

Weil, Thomas, et al. *Area Handbook for the Dominican Republic.* Washington, D.C.: U.S. Government Printing Office, 1973.

Williams, Eric. *From Columbus to Castro: The History of the Caribbean, 1492–1969.* New York: Harper and Row, 1970.

———. *The Negro in the Caribbean.* New York: Negro Universities Press, 1942.

Williams, Lorna V. "From Dusky Venus to Mater Dolorosa: The Female Protagonist in the Cuban Antislavery Novel." In *Woman as Myth and Metaphor in Latin American Literature,* edited by Carmelo Virgillo and Naomi Lindstrom, 121–35. Columbia: University of Missouri Press, 1985.

———. *Self and Society in the Poetry of Nicolás Guillén.* Baltimore: Johns Hopkins University Press, 1982.

Williams, Raymond. *Marxism and Literature.* London: Oxford University Press, 1977.

Wolf, Donna M. "The *Cuban Gente de Color* and the Independence Movement, 1879–1895." *Revista/Review interamericana* 5 (1975): 403–21.

Wolff, Janet. *The Social Production of Art.* New York: New York University Press, 1984.

Woolcock, Joseph. "Politics, Ideology, and Hegemony in Gramsci's Theory." *Social and Economic Studies* [Institute of Social and Economic Research, University of the West Indies, Jamaica] 34 (1985): 199–210.

Wynter, Sylvia. "The Eye of the Other: Images of the Black in Spanish Literature." In *Blacks in Hispanic Literature: Critical Essays,* edited by Miriam DeCosta, 8–19. Port Washington, N.Y.: Kennikat Press, 1977.

Young, Ann Venture. "The Black Woman in Afro-Caribbean Poetry." In *Blacks in Hispanic Literature: Critical Essays,* edited by Miriam DeCosta, 137–42. Port Washington, N.Y.: Kennikat Press, 1977.

———. "Black Women in Hispanic American Poetry: Glorification, Deification, and Humanization." *Afro-Hispanic Review* 1, no. 1 (1982): 23–28.

———, ed. *The Image of the Black Woman in Twentieth-Century South American Poetry. A Bilingual Anthology.* Washington, D.C.: Three Continents Press, 1987.

Zambrana, Antonio. *El negro Francisco.* 1873; rpt. Havana: P. Fernandez y Cia., 1951.

Zenón Cruz, Isabelo. *Narciso descubre su trasero.* Vol. 2. Humaco, Puerto Rico: Editorial Furidi, 1974.

INDEX